1798 DIRECT TAX
NEW HAMPSHIRE DISTRICT #13

Consisting of the Towns of

Alton, Brookfield, Effingham, Middleton,
New Durham, Ossipee, Tuftonboro,
Wakefield, and Wolfeboro

Transcribed from the Original Schedules by

John S. Fipphen

HERITAGE BOOKS
2020

HERITAGE BOOKS
AN IMPRINT OF HERITAGE BOOKS, INC.

Books, CDs, and more—Worldwide

For our listing of thousands of titles see our website at
www.HeritageBooks.com

Published 2020 by
HERITAGE BOOKS, INC.
Publishing Division
5810 Ruatan Street
Berwyn Heights, Md. 20740

Copyright © 1988 Wolfeboro Historical Society

Heritage Books by John S. Fipphen:
*1798 Direct Tax New Hampshire District #13, Consisting of the Towns of
Alton, Brookfield, Effingham, Middleton, New Durham, Ossipee, Tuftonboro, Wakefield, and Wolfeboro*
Cemetery Inscriptions, Wolfeboro, New Hampshire

All rights reserved. No part of this book may be reproduced or transmitted in any form or by any means, electronic or mechanical, including photocopying, recording or by any information storage and retrieval system without written permission from the author, except for the inclusion of brief quotations in a review.

International Standard Book Numbers
Paperbound: 978-1-55613-259-9
Clothbound: 978-0-7884-9063-7

FOREWORD

In 1798, France was raiding American shipping off the American coast, the English coast, as well as the islands of the West Indies. As a result, relations between the new Federal government of the United States and the new Directorate regime of France deteriorated to the point where the French would not receive the three American commissioners sent to Paris by President John Adams to negotiate a settlement of differences. France, through three unofficial envoys, demanded that America pay fifty thousand pounds just to deal with the French government. The three French envoys were referred to as Mr. X, Mr. Y, and Mr. Z by President Adams; hence, this incident became known as the "X Y Z Affair." Members of Congress, infuriated at the solicitation of a bribe, coined the slogan "Millions for defense, but not one cent for tribute."

Congress passed many acts including one to establish a navy and an army. To provide the necessary funds, a direct tax on real property was levied throughout the states. This levy resulted in extensive names and property lists; this document is one of these lists.

The discovery of these original schedules is significant because the 1800 Federal Census schedules covering the nine towns encompassed by this tax list have been lost. (<u>Heads of Families at 2nd Census of the United States taken in the year 1800, New Hampshire</u>, by John Brooks Threfall, Madison, Wisconsin, 1973.)

The document was, at some time in the past, placed in a customized plywood box. It is in good condition, considering its age. It is apparent, however, that there are missing pages. For example, the end of the "E" Schedule is not signed by the commissioners for the State of New Hampshire as is the end of the "D" Schedule. Examination of the binding reveals the probable existence of two additional pages in the front and two more in the back. The binding also shows evidence that there was a leather cover over the document. This cover is also missing. The document is now in an archival box in a climate-controlled environment.

This transcription has been done according to the actual listing. Hence, the reader may note inconsistent spellings, which were used by the scriveners of the original document.

ACKNOWLEDGEMENTS

I wish to thank Harrison Moore, a local historian in Wolfeboro, who brought the original schedules to my attention. I would like to give special thanks to the members of the Wolfeboro Historical Society for their enthusiastic support and keen interest in the completion of the transcription of these schedules. I would also give special thanks to my wife, Christine Fipphen, for hours of patient proof-reading to ensure the accuracy of the text and for countless helpful ideas.

John S. Fipphen
Wolfeboro, New Hampshire
December, 1988

SCHEDULE D

GENERAL LIST Of all Dwelling-Houses which, with the Out-Houses appurtenant thereto, and the Lots on which the same are erected, not exceeding Two Acres in any case, were Owned, Possessed or Occupied on the First Day of October 1798, within Assessment District No. 13 in the State of New Hampshire, exceeding in value the sum of One Hundred Dollars.

The headings of each column are as follows:
    Page and Number of particular entry.
    Names of Possessors or Occupants.
    Names of Reputed Owners.
    Number of Dwelling Houses &c. exempted from Valuation.
        Dwelling Houses.
        Outhouses.
        Quantity of Land in Lots.
            Acres.
            Perches.
            Sqr. Ft.
    Number of Dwelling Houses &c. subject to and included in the Valuation.
        Dwelling Houses.
        Out Houses.
        Quantities of Land in Lots valued therewith.
            Acres.
            Perches
            Sqr. Ft.
   In what Township or Parish in the Assessment District situated.
    Place of Residence of the Reputed owners.
    Valuation as determined by the Principal Assessors.
       Dollars.
       Cents.
    Rate percentum of 25 addition prescribed by the Commissioners.
    Valuation as revised and equalized by the Commissioners.
       Dollars.
       Cents.

Editor's note: Because of space constraints, the Sqr. Ft. columns were not included in this transcription since there are no square feet values entered in the original record. The first two digits for each line represent the page number of the schedule and the last 2 digits represent the line number on the page.

1798 DIRECT TAX

Pg/ No.	Occupant Surname	Occupant First Name	Owner Surname	Owner First Name	Exempt Dwg	Exempt Acr	Exempt Per
101	Allen	Ebenezer	Allen	Ebenezer	1	1	-
102	Allard	Henry	Allard	Henry	-	-	-
103	Bassett	Daniel	Bassett	Daniel	-	-	-
104	Bickford	Jonathan	Bickford	Jonathan	-	-	-
105	Blake	Benj. & Jonathan	Blake	Benj. & Jonathan	-	-	-
106	Brown	Moses	Brown	Moses	-	-	-
107	Brown	Nathaniel	Brown	Nathaniel	-	-	-
108	Brewster	George	Brewster	George	-	-	-
109	Chase	Thomas	Chase	Thomas	-	-	-
110	Connor	James	Connor	James	-	-	-
111	Copp	David	Copp	David	-	-	-
112	Cotton	Thomas	Cotton	Thomas	-	-	-
113	Cotton	William	Cotton	William	-	-	-
114	Estes	Samuel	Estes	Samuel	-	-	-
115	Fernald	James	Fernald	James	-	-	-
116	Frost	Aaron	Frost	Aaron	-	-	-
117	Fullerton	James	Fullerton	James	-	-	-
118	Furber	John	Furber	John	-	-	-
119	Fullerton	John	Fullerton	John	-	-	-
201	Hardy	Dudly	Hardy	Dudly	-	-	-
202	Haines	Jacob	Haines	Jacob	-	-	-
203	Haines	Joseph	Haines	Joseph	-	-	-
204	Haines	Joshua	Haines	Joshua	-	-	-
205	Hersey	Jonathan	Hersey	Jonathan	-	-	-
206	Hide	Samuel	Hide	Samuel	-	-	-
207	Horn	Benjamin	Horn	Benjamin	-	-	-
208	Horn	Isaiah	Horn	Isaiah	-	-	-
209	Horn	John	Horn	John	-	-	-
210	Horn	Stephen	Horn	Stephen	-	-	-
211	Jewett	Andrew	Jewett	Andrew	-	-	-
212	Adams	Asa	Lane	George	-	-	-
213	Brown	Nathaniel	Lane	George	-	-	-
214	Libbey	Reuben	Libbey	Reuben	-	-	-
215	Meder	Ebenezer	Meder	Ebenezer	-	-	-
216	Rogers	William	Rogers	William	-	-	-
217	Rust	Henry	Rust	Henry	-	-	-
218	Rust	Henry, Jr.	Rust	Henry, Jr.	-	-	-
219	Rust	Richard	Rust	Richard	-	-	-
220	Smith	Jacob	Smith	Jacob	-	-	-
221	Tibbets	Levi & Benj.	Tibbets	Levi & Benj.	-	-	-
222	Townsend	Isaac	Townsend	Isaac	-	-	-
223	Trask	Hannah	Trask	Hannah	-	-	-
224	Triggs	William	Triggs	William	-	-	-
225	Thurston	Moses	Thurston	Moses	-	-	-
226	Verney	Joseph	Verney	Joseph	-	-	-
301	Warren	George	Warren	George	-	-	-
302	Whittle	Thomas	Whittle	Thomas	-	-	-

NEW HAMPSHIRE DISTRICT 13

Pg/No.	Dwg	Out Hou	Acr	Per	Property Location	Residence of Owner	Value $	Eq Val $
101	-	-	-	-	Wolfeboro	Wolfeboro	-	-
102	1	-	-	80	Wolfeboro	Wolfeboro	105.60	132.00
103	1	-	-	40	Wolfeboro	Wolfeboro	100.20	125.25
104	1	-	-	80	Wolfeboro	Wolfeboro	130.00	162.50
105	1	-	-	80	Wolfeboro	Wolfeboro	180.00	225.00
106	1	-	-	80	Wolfeboro	Wolfeboro	150.00	187.50
107	1	-	-	80	Wolfeboro	Wolfeboro	150.00	187.50
108	1	-	-	80	Wolfeboro	Wolfeboro	100.00	125.00
109	1	-	-	80	Wolfeboro	Wolfeboro	125.20	156.50
110	1	-	-	80	Wolfeboro	Wolfeboro	160.00	200.00
111	1	-	-	80	Wolfeboro	Wolfeboro	150.00	187.50
112	1	-	-	80	Wolfeboro	Wolfeboro	100.60	125.75
113	1	-	-	80	Wolfeboro	Wolfeboro	200.00	250.00
114	1	-	-	80	Wolfeboro	Wolfeboro	106.20	132.75
115	1	-	-	80	Wolfeboro	Wolfeboro	130.00	162.50
116	1	-	-	80	Wolfeboro	Wolfeboro	130.00	162.50
117	1	-	-	80	Wolfeboro	Wolfeboro	130.00	162.50
118	1	-	-	80	Wolfeboro	Wolfeboro	200.00	250.00
119	1	-	-	80	Wolfeboro	Wolfeboro	200.00	250.00
201	1	-	-	80	Wolfeboro	Wolfeboro	170.00	212.50
202	1	-	-	80	Wolfeboro	Wolfeboro	100.60	125.75
203	1	-	-	80	Wolfeboro	Wolfeboro	100.60	125.75
204	1	-	-	80	Wolfeboro	Wolfeboro	170.00	212.50
205	1	-	-	80	Wolfeboro	Wolfeboro	260.00	325.00
206	1	-	-	80	Wolfeboro	Wolfeboro	150.60	188.25
207	1	-	-	80	Wolfeboro	Wolfeboro	120.00	150.00
208	1	-	-	80	Wolfeboro	Wolfeboro	300.00	375.00
209	1	-	-	80	Wolfeboro	Wolfeboro	100.20	125.25
210	1	-	-	80	Wolfeboro	Wolfeboro	170.00	212.50
211	1	-	-	40	Wolfeboro	Wolfeboro	150.00	187.50
212	1	-	-	80	Wolfeboro	Charterton, MA	500.00	625.00
213	1	1	1	-	Wolfeboro	Charterton, MA	300.00	375.00
214	1	-	-	80	Wolfeboro	Wolfeboro	200.00	250.00
215	1	-	-	80	Wolfeboro	Wolfeboro	180.00	225.00
216	1	-	-	80	Wolfeboro	Wolfeboro	180.00	225.00
217	1	-	-	80	Wolfeboro	Wolfeboro	160.00	200.00
218	1	-	-	80	Wolfeboro	Wolfeboro	120.00	150.00
219	1	-	-	80	Wolfeboro	Wolfeboro	230.00	287.50
220	1	-	-	80	Wolfeboro	Wolfeboro	100.20	125.25
221	1	-	-	80	Wolfeboro	Wolfeboro	150.00	187.50
222	1	-	-	80	Wolfeboro	Wolfeboro	150.00	187.50
223	1	-	-	80	Wolfeboro	Wolfeboro	200.00	250.00
224	1	-	-	80	Wolfeboro	Wolfeboro	120.00	150.00
225	1	-	-	80	Wolfeboro	Wolfeboro	106.00	132.50
226	1	-	-	80	Wolfeboro	Wolfeboro	160.00	200.00
301	1	-	-	80	Wolfeboro	Wolfeboro	100.60	125.75
302	1	-	-	80	Wolfeboro	Wolfeboro	175.00	218.75

1798 DIRECT TAX

Pg/No.	Occupant Surname	Occupant First Name	Owner Surname	Owner First Name	Exempt Dwg	Exempt Acr	Exempt Per
303	Wiggin	Andrew	Wiggin	Andrew	-	-	-
304	Wiggin	Paul	Wiggin	Paul	-	-	-
305	Young	John	Young	John	-	-	-
306	Copp	William	Copp	William	-	-	-
307	Dearborn	Joseph	Dearborn	Joseph	-	-	-
308	Graves	Phineas	Graves	Phineas	-	-	-
309	Wiggin	Henry & Henry Jr	Wiggin	Henry & Henry Jr	-	-	-
310	Allen	Abner	Allen	Abner	-	-	-
311	Allen	Samuel	Allen	Samuel	-	-	-
312	Ballard	Frederick	Ballard	Frederick	-	-	-
313	Blasdel	William W.	Blasdel	William W.	-	-	-
314	Burley	Jonathan	Burley	Jonathan	-	-	-
315	Calder	Robert	Calder	Robert	-	-	-
316	Chapman	Samuel	Chapman	Samuel	-	-	-
317	Cook	Nathaniel	Cook	Nathaniel	-	-	-
318	Cook	Peter	Cook	Peter	-	-	-
319	Clark	Jacob	Clark	Jacob	-	-	-
320	Cloutman	Thomas	Cloutman	Thomas	-	-	-
321	Copp	David	Copp	David	-	-	-
322	Dearborn	Benjamin	Dearborn	Benjamin	-	-	-
323	Dearborn	Zeriah	Dearborn	Zeriah	-	-	-
324	Dow	Richard	Dow	Richard	-	-	-
325	Garland	John	Garland	John	-	-	-
326	Gilman	Andrew	Gilman	Andrew	-	-	-
401	Gilman	John	Gilman	John	-	-	-
402	Hall	Avery	Hall	Avery	-	-	-
403	Hall	Daniel	Hall	Daniel	-	-	-
404	Hanson	Tobias	Hanson	Tobias	-	-	-
405	Haines	Joseph	Haines	Joseph	-	-	-
406	Hardy	Robert	Hardy	Robert	-	-	-
407	Horn	John	Horn	John	-	-	-
408	Hutchens	James	Hutchens	James	-	-	-
409	Hutchens	Solomon	Hutchens	Solomon	-	-	-
410	Kimball	John	Kimball	John	-	-	-
411	Kimball	Noah	Kimball	Noah	-	-	-
412	Lang	Reuben	Lang	Reuben	-	-	-
413	Leavitt	Joseph	Leavitt	Joseph	-	-	-
414	Lindsey	Thomas	Lindsey	Thomas	-	-	-
415	Unoccupied	-	Manning	John	-	-	-
416	Mailham	Joseph	Mailham	Joseph	-	-	-
417	Mordough	Robert	Mordough	Robert	-	-	-
418	Neal	Levi	Neal	Levi	-	-	-
419	Nudd	Thomas, Jr.	Nudd	Thomas, Jr.	-	-	-
420	Perkins	Daniel	Perkins	Daniel	-	-	-
421	Palmer	Jonathan	Palmer	Jonathan	-	-	-
422	Philbrick	Eliphalet	Philbrick	Eliphalet	-	-	-
423	Piper	Asa	Piper	Asa	1	-	80

NEW HAMPSHIRE DISTRICT 13

Pg/No.	Dwg	Out Hou	Acr	Per	Property Location	Residence of Owner	Value $	Eq Val $
303	1	-	-	80	Wolfeboro	Wolfeboro	120.00	150.00
304	1	-	-	80	Wolfeboro	Wolfeboro	100.20	125.25
305	1	-	-	80	Wolfeboro	Wolfeboro	300.00	375.00
306	1	-	1	-	Tuftonboro	Tuftonboro	150.00	187.50
307	1	-	1	-	Tuftonboro	Tuftonboro	130.00	162.50
308	1	-	1	-	Tuftonboro	Tuftonboro	130.00	162.50
309	1	-	1	-	Tuftonboro	Tuftonboro	350.00	437.50
310	1	-	-	80	Wakefield	Wakefield	160.00	200.00
311	1	-	-	40	Wakefield	Wakefield	150.00	187.50
312	1	-	1	-	Wakefield	Wakefield	150.00	187.50
313	1	-	1	-	Wakefield	Wakefield	150.00	187.50
314	1	-	-	80	Wakefield	Wakefield	150.00	187.50
315	1	-	-	11	Wakefield	Wakefield	-	-
316	1	-	-	40	Wakefield	Wakefield	130.00	162.50
317	1	-	1	-	Wakefield	Wakefield	110.00	137.50
318	1	-	1	-	Wakefield	Wakefield	110.00	137.50
319	1	-	1	-	Wakefield	Wakefield	450.00	562.50
320	1	-	-	40	Wakefield	Wakefield	110.00	137.50
321	1	-	1	-	Wakefield	Wakefield	110.00	137.50
322	1	-	1	-	Wakefield	Wakefield	300.00	375.00
323	1	-	1	-	Wakefield	Wakefield	220.00	275.00
324	1	-	-	80	Wakefield	Wakefield	200.00	250.00
325	1	-	-	40	Wakefield	Wakefield	150.00	187.50
326	1	-	-	80	Wakefield	Wakefield	180.00	225.00
401	1	-	-	80	Wakefield	Wakefield	300.00	375.00
402	1	-	-	80	Wakefield	Wakefield	210.00	262.50
403	1	-	-	40	Wakefield	Wakefield	140.00	175.00
404	1	-	-	80	Wakefield	Wakefield	170.00	212.50
405	1	-	-	40	Wakefield	Wakefield	105.00	131.25
406	1	-	-	40	Wakefield	Wakefield	105.00	131.25
407	1	-	-	6	Wakefield	Wakefield	120.00	150.00
408	1	-	-	20	Wakefield	Wakefield	120.00	150.00
409	1	-	-	40	Wakefield	Wakefield	180.00	225.00
410	1	-	-	80	Wakefield	Wakefield	150.00	187.50
411	1	-	1	-	Wakefield	Wakefield	340.00	425.00
412	1	-	1	-	Wakefield	Wakefield	130.00	162.50
413	1	1	1	-	Wakefield	Wakefield	315.00	393.75
414	1	-	1	-	Wakefield	Wakefield	120.00	150.00
415	2	-	1	-	Wakefield	Wakefield	240.00	300.00
416	1	-	1	-	Wakefield	Wakefield	150.00	187.50
417	1	-	-	80	Wakefield	Wakefield	150.00	187.50
418	1	-	-	-	Wakefield	Wakefield	160.00	200.00
419	1	-	-	80	Wakefield	Wakefield	150.00	187.50
420	1	-	-	40	Wakefield	Wakefield	120.00	150.00
421	1	-	1	-	Wakefield	Wakefield	800.00	1000.00
422	1	-	-	40	Wakefield	Wakefield	180.00	225.00
423	-	-	-	-	Wakefield	Wakefield	-	-

1798 DIRECT TAX

Pg/No.	Occupant Surname	Occupant First Name	Owner Surname	Owner First Name	Exempt Dwg	Exempt Acr	Exempt Per
424	Sanborn	Elisha	Sanborn	Elisha	-	-	-
425	Sawyer	Timothy	Sawyer	Timothy	-	-	-
426	Seammon	Hezekiah	Seammon	Hezekiah	-	-	-
501	Skinner	Christopher	Skinner	Christopher	-	-	-
502	Watson	Stephen	Watson	Stephen	-	-	-
503	Wingate	John	Wingate	John	-	-	-
504	Welch	Jacob	Welch	Jacob	-	-	-
505	Wiggin	Henry	Wiggin	Henry	-	-	-
506	Weeks	John	Weeks	John	-	-	-
507	Young	James	Young	James	-	-	-
508	Cook	Joseph	Cook	Joseph	-	-	-
509	Davis	John	Davis	John	-	-	-
510	Frost	Samuel	Frost	Samuel	-	-	-
511	Hiner	John H.	Hiner	John H.	-	-	-
512	Pike	Henry	Pike	Henry	-	-	-
513	Pike	Jacob	Pike	Jacob	-	-	-
514	Wingate	Daniel	Wingate	Daniel	-	-	-
515	Baker	Thomas	Baker	Thomas	-	-	-
516	Calder	Robert	Calder	Robert	-	-	-
517	Chappotin	Leon	Chappotin	Leon	-	-	-
518	Clay	Benjamin	Clay	Benjamin	-	-	-
519	Chamberlain	James	Chamberlain	James	-	-	-
520	Chamberlain	Thomas	Chamberlain	Thomas	-	-	-
521	Chamberlain	William	Chamberlain	William	-	-	-
522	Colman	Mary	Colman	Mary	-	-	-
523	Drew	Andrew	Drew	Andrew	-	-	-
524	Fernald	John	Fernald	John	-	-	-
525	Guppy	Joshua	Guppy	Joshua	-	-	-
526	Hodge	Hiram	Hackett	James	-	-	-
601	Hanson	Richard	Hanson	Richard	-	-	-
602	Johnson	Phineas	Johnson	Phineas	-	-	-
603	Johnson	Timothy	Johnson	Timothy	-	-	-
604	Kennison	Waldron	Kennison	Waldron	-	-	-
605	Lyford	Stephen	Lyford	Stephen	-	-	-
606	Martin	John	Martin	John	-	-	-
607	Robinson	Tristram	Robinson	Tristram	-	-	-
608	Stanton	Charles	Stanton	Charles	-	-	-
609	Sanborn	Ezekiel	Sanborn	Ezekiel	-	-	-
610	Sayer	Michael	Sayer	Michael	-	-	-
611	Stodard	Deering	Stodard	Deering	-	-	-
612	Tibbets	Samuel	Tibbets	Samuel	-	-	-
613	Watson	Nathan	Watson	Nathan	-	-	-
614	Whitehouse	Moses	Whitehouse	Moses	-	-	-
615	Wiggin	Josiah	Wiggin	Josiah	-	-	-
616	Tasker	Ebenezer	Brown	Simon	-	-	-
617	Dearborn	Asahel	Dearborn	Asahel	-	-	-
618	Dearborn	Benjamin	Dearborn	Benjamin	-	-	-

NEW HAMPSHIRE DISTRICT 13

Pg/No.	Dwg	Out Hou	Acr	Per	Property Location	Residence of Owner	Value $	Eq Val $
424	1	-	-	-	Wakefield	Wakefield	175.00	218.75
425	1	-	-	80	Wakefield	Wakefield	300.00	375.00
426	1	-	-	80	Wakefield	Wakefield	150.00	187.50
501	1	-	1	-	Wakefield	Wakefield	200.00	250.00
502	1	-	-	80	Wakefield	Wakefield	230.00	287.50
503	1	-	1	-	Wakefield	Wakefield	120.00	150.00
504	1	-	-	80	Wakefield	Wakefield	105.00	131.25
505	1	-	-	80	Wakefield	Wakefield	140.00	175.00
506	1	-	-	80	Wakefield	Wakefield	110.00	137.50
507	1	-	-	40	Wakefield	Wakefield	130.00	162.50
508	1	-	-	80	Middleton	Middleton	190.00	237.50
509	1	-	-	80	Middleton	Middleton	130.00	162.50
510	1	-	-	80	Middleton	Middleton	170.00	212.50
511	1	-	-	80	Middleton	Middleton	150.00	187.50
512	1	-	-	80	Middleton	Middleton	130.00	162.50
513	1	-	-	80	Middleton	Middleton	150.00	187.50
514	1	-	-	80	Middleton	Middleton	200.00	250.00
515	1	-	-	80	Brookfield	Brookfield	120.00	150.00
516	1	-	-	80	Brookfield	Brookfield	140.00	175.00
517	1	-	-	80	Brookfield	Brookfield	130.00	162.50
518	1	-	-	80	Brookfield	Brookfield	180.00	225.00
519	1	-	-	80	Brookfield	Brookfield	230.00	287.50
520	1	-	-	80	Brookfield	Brookfield	200.00	250.00
521	1	-	-	80	Brookfield	Brookfield	320.00	400.00
522	1	-	-	80	Brookfield	Brookfield	250.00	312.50
523	1	-	-	80	Brookfield	Brookfield	160.00	200.00
524	1	-	-	80	Brookfield	Brookfield	130.00	162.50
525	1	-	-	80	Brookfield	Brookfield	120.00	150.00
526	1	-	-	80	Brookfield	Piscataqua Isle	400.00	500.00
601	1	-	-	80	Brookfield	Brookfield	420.00	525.00
602	1	-	-	80	Brookfield	Brookfield	180.00	225.00
603	1	-	-	80	Brookfield	Brookfield	160.00	200.00
604	1	-	-	80	Brookfield	Brookfield	200.00	250.00
605	1	-	-	80	Brookfield	Brookfield	150.00	187.50
606	1	-	-	80	Brookfield	Brookfield	110.00	137.50
607	1	-	-	80	Brookfield	Brookfield	110.00	137.50
608	1	-	-	80	Brookfield	Brookfield	140.00	175.00
609	1	-	-	80	Brookfield	Brookfield	150.00	187.50
610	1	-	-	80	Brookfield	Brookfield	125.00	156.25
611	1	-	-	80	Brookfield	Brookfield	120.00	150.00
612	1	-	-	80	Brookfield	Brookfield	120.00	150.00
613	1	-	-	80	Brookfield	Brookfield	180.00	225.00
614	1	-	-	80	Brookfield	Brookfield	190.00	237.50
615	1	-	-	80	Brookfield	Brookfield	120.00	150.00
616	1	-	-	80	Effingham	North Hampton	150.00	187.50
617	1	-	-	80	Effingham	Effingham	270.00	337.50
618	1	-	-	40	Effingham	Effingham	100.20	125.25

1798 DIRECT TAX

Pg/No.	Occupant Surname	Occupant First Name	Owner Surname	Owner First Name	Exempt Dwg	Exempt Acr	Exempt Per
619	Drake	Abraham	Drake	Abraham	-	-	-
620	Drake	John Jr.	Drake	John Jr.	-	-	-
621	Hobbs	Benjamin	Hobbs	Benjamin	-	-	-
622	Hobbs	Nathaniel	Hobbs	Nathaniel	-	-	-
623	Leavitt	Carr	Leavitt	Carr	-	-	-
624	Lord	Isaac	Lord	Isaac	-	-	-
625	Marston	Abraham	Marston	Abraham	-	-	-
626	Moulton	Redman	Moulton	Redman	-	-	-
701	Philbrick	Simon	Philbrick	Simon	-	-	-
702	Taylor	John Jr.	Taylor	John Jr.	-	-	-
703	Titcomb	James	Titcomb	James	-	-	-
704	Titcomb	Joshua	Titcomb	Joshua	-	-	-
705	Bennett	John Jr.	Bennett	John Jr.	-	-	-
706	Berry	Benjamin	Berry	Benjamin	-	-	-
707	Berry	Joseph	Berry	Joseph	-	-	-
708	Bickford	Abraham	Bickford	Abraham	-	-	-
709	Bickford	John	Bickford	John	-	-	-
710	Boody	Zachariah	Boody	Zachariah	-	-	-
711	Canney	John	Canney	John	-	-	-
712	Chamberlain	Abraham	Chamberlain	Abraham	-	-	-
713	Colomy	John	Colomy	John	-	-	-
714	Davis	Ebenezer	Davis	Ebenezer	-	-	-
715	Davis	Elisha	Davis	Elisha	-	-	-
716	Davis	George	Davis	George	-	-	-
717	Davis	John	Davis	John	-	-	-
718	Davis	Solomon	Davis	Solomon	-	-	-
719	Davis	Winthrop	Davis	Winthrop	-	-	-
720	Drew	Solomon	Drew	Solomon	-	-	-
721	Durgan	Daniel	Durgan	Daniel	-	-	-
722	Durgan	Lydia	Durgin	Lydia	-	-	-
723	Edgerly	Caleb	Edgerly	Caleb	-	-	-
724	Edgerly	Josiah	Edgerly	Josiah	-	-	-
725	Elkins	David	Elkins	David	-	-	-
726	Folsom	Jonathan	Folsom	Jonathan	-	-	-
801	French	Thomas	French	Thomas	-	-	-
802	Cogswell	Joseph	Jaffrey	George	-	-	-
803	Jackson	Joseph	Jackson	Joseph	-	-	-
804	Jennings	Richard	Jennings	Richard	-	-	-
805	Joy	Samuel	Joy	Samuel	-	-	-
806	Kineson	Nathan	Kineson	Nathan	-	-	-
807	Leighton	Jacob	Leighton	Jacob	-	-	-
808	Mooney	Joseph	Mooney	Joseph	-	-	-
809	Roberts	John	Roberts	John	-	-	-
810	Runnals	Samuel	Runnals	Samuel	-	-	-
811	Stevens	Durrel	Stevens	Durrel	-	-	-
812	Tash	Thomas	Tash	Thomas	-	-	-
813	Wille	Benjamin	Wille	Benjamin	-	-	-

NEW HAMPSHIRE DISTRICT 13

Pg/No.	Dwg	Out Hou	Acr	Per	Property Location	Residence of Owner	Value $	Eq Val $
619	1	-	-	80	Effingham	Effingham	350.00	437.50
620	1	-	-	40	Effingham	Effingham	150.00	187.50
621	1	-	-	80	Effingham	Effingham	140.00	175.00
622	1	1	-	80	Effingham	Effingham	150.00	187.50
623	1	-	-	80	Effingham	Effingham	300.00	375.00
624	1	-	-	40	Effingham	Effingham	250.00	312.50
625	1	-	-	40	Effingham	Effingham	150.00	187.50
626	1	-	-	80	Effingham	Effingham	160.00	200.00
701	1	-	-	40	Effingham	Effingham	120.00	150.00
702	1	-	-	80	Effingham	Effingham	220.00	275.00
703	1	-	-	40	Effingham	Effingham	100.20	125.25
704	1	-	-	40	Effingham	Effingham	160.00	200.00
705	1	-	1	-	New Durham	New Durham	220.00	275.00
706	1	-	1	-	New Durham	New Durham	140.00	175.00
707	1	-	1	-	New Durham	New Durham	105.00	131.25
708	1	-	1	-	New Durham	New Durham	125.00	156.25
709	1	-	1	-	New Durham	New Durham	130.00	162.50
710	1	-	1	-	New Durham	New Durham	220.00	275.00
711	1	-	-	80	New Durham	New Durham	150.00	187.50
712	1	-	1	-	New Durham	New Durham	125.00	156.25
713	1	1	1	-	New Durham	New Durham	460.00	575.00
714	1	-	1	-	New Durham	New Durham	260.00	325.00
715	1	-	1	-	New Durham	New Durham	350.00	437.50
716	1	-	-	80	New Durham	New Durham	120.00	150.00
717	1	-	-	80	New Durham	New Durham	110.00	137.50
718	1	-	-	80	New Durham	New Durham	130.00	162.50
719	1	-	-	80	New Durham	New Durham	140.00	175.00
720	1	-	-	80	New Durham	New Durham	180.00	225.00
721	1	-	-	80	New Durham	New Durham	110.00	137.50
722	1	-	1	-	New Durham	New Durham	220.00	275.00
723	1	-	1	-	New Durham	New Durham	140.00	175.00
724	1	-	1	-	New Durham	New Durham	220.00	275.00
725	1	-	-	80	New Durham	New Durham	220.00	275.00
726	1	-	-	80	New Durham	New Durham	105.00	131.25
801	1	-	-	80	New Durham	New Durham	130.00	162.50
802	1	-	1	-	New Durham	Portsmouth	200.00	250.00
803	1	-	-	80	New Durham	New Durham	120.00	150.00
804	1	2	-	40	New Durham	New Durham	250.00	312.50
805	1	-	-	80	New Durham	New Durham	110.00	137.50
806	1	-	-	80	New Durham	New Durham	100.20	125.25
807	1	-	-	80	New Durham	New Durham	130.00	162.50
808	1	-	1	-	New Durham	New Durham	230.00	287.50
809	1	-	-	80	New Durham	New Durham	100.20	125.25
810	1	-	1	-	New Durham	New Durham	230.00	287.50
811	1	-	-	80	New Durham	New Durham	210.00	262.50
812	1	-	1	-	New Durham	New Durham	200.00	250.00
813	1	-	-	80	New Durham	New Durham	130.00	162.50

1798 DIRECT TAX

Pg/No.	Occupant Surname	Occupant First Name	Owner Surname	Owner First Name	Exempt Dwg	Acr	Per
814	Wille	Joseph L.	Wille	Joseph L.	-	-	-
815	Wille	Samuel Jr.	Wille	Samuel Jr.	-	-	-
816	Brown	Jacob	Brown	Jacob	-	-	-
817	Dodge	Jonathan	Dodge	Jonathan	-	-	-
818	Fogg	Joseph	Fogg	Joseph	-	-	-
819	Fogg	Seth	Fogg	Seth	-	-	-
820	Folson	Andrew	Folsom	Andrew	-	-	-
821	Knight	Ephraim	Knight	Ephraim	-	-	-
822	Nay	Joseph	Nay	Joseph	-	-	-
823	Poland	Josiah	Poland	Josiah	-	-	-
824	Sias	Eliphalet	Sias	Eliphalet	-	-	-
825	Smith	Samuel	Smith	Samuel	-	-	-
826	Young	John	Young	John	-	-	-
901	Bennett	Benjamin	Bennett	Benjamin	-	-	-
902	Bean	Joel	Bean	Joel	-	-	-
903	Buzzell	Joseph	Buzzell	Joseph	-	-	-
904	Chamberlain	Ephraim	Chamberlain	Ephraim	-	-	-
905	Chamberlain	Jacob	Chamberlain	Jacob	-	-	-
906	Chamberlain	Paul	Chamberlain	Paul	-	-	-
907	Coffin	Jonathan	Coffin	Jonathan	-	-	-
908	Clough	Perley	Clough	Perley	-	-	-
909	Davis	Eleazer	Davis	Eleazer	-	-	-
910	Davis	Gideon	Davis	Gideon	-	-	-
911	Pinkham	Stephen	Davis	Gideon	-	-	-
912	Davis	Timothy	Davis	Timothy	-	-	-
913	Davis	Hezekiah	Davis	Hezekiah	-	-	-
914	Davis	Zebulon	Davis	Zebulon	-	-	-
915	Dudley	Daniel	Dudley	Daniel	-	-	-
916	Dudley	Stephen	Dudley	Stephen	-	-	-
917	Clough	Samuel	Fisher	John	-	-	-
918	Flanders	Ezekiel	Flanders	Ezekiel	-	-	-
919	Flanders	Thomas	Flanders	Thomas	-	-	-
920	Folsom	John	Folsom	John	-	-	-
921	Gilman	Moses	Gilman	Moses	-	-	-
922	Glidden	David	Glidden	David	-	-	-
923	Glidden	John	Glidden	John	-	-	-
924	Hanson	Micaiah	Hanson	Micaiah	-	-	-
925	-	-	Hayes	Joseph	-	-	-
926	Hayes	Paul	Hayes	Paul	-	-	-
1001	Jewett	Thomas	Jewett	Thomas	-	-	-
1002	Wilkinson	James	Jewett	James	-	-	-
1003	Wooster	James	Jewett	James	-	-	-
1004	Hayes	Jonathan	Jewett	Jervis	-	-	-
1005	McDuffee	Daniel	McDuffee	Daniel	-	-	-
1006	McDuffee	Jonathan	McDuffee	Jonathan	-	-	-
1007	McDuffee	James	McDuffee	James	-	-	-
1008	Morrison	David	Morrison	David	-	-	-

NEW HAMPSHIRE DISTRICT 13

Pg/No.	Dwg	Out Hou	Acr	Per	Property Location	Residence of Owner	Value $	Eq Val $
814	1	-	-	80	New Durham	New Durham	100.20	125.25
815	1	-	-	80	New Durham	New Durham	220.00	275.00
816	1	-	1	-	Ossipee	Ossipee	150.00	187.50
817	1	1	1	-	Ossipee	Ossipee	220.00	275.00
818	1	-	1	-	Ossipee	Ossipee	170.00	212.50
819	1	-	1	-	Ossipee	Ossipee	250.00	312.50
820	1	-	1	-	Ossipee	Ossipee	230.00	287.50
821	1	-	1	-	Ossipee	Ossipee	180.00	225.00
822	1	-	1	-	Ossipee	Ossipee	150.00	187.50
823	1	-	1	-	Ossipee	Ossipee	160.00	200.00
824	1	-	1	-	Ossipee	Ossipee	130.00	162.50
825	1	-	1	-	Ossipee	Ossipee	130.00	162.50
826	1	-	1	-	Ossipee	Ossipee	120.00	150.00
901	1	-	-	80	Alton	Alton	160.00	200.00
902	1	-	-	80	Alton	Alton	200.00	250.00
903	1	-	-	40	Alton	Alton	160.00	200.00
904	1	-	-	40	Alton	Alton	200.00	250.00
905	1	-	1	-	Alton	Alton	320.00	400.00
906	1	-	-	40	Alton	Alton	100.60	125.75
907	1	-	1	-	Alton	Alton	360.00	450.00
908	1	-	-	40	Alton	Alton	120.00	150.00
909	1	-	1	-	Alton	Alton	360.00	450.00
910	1	-	1	-	Alton	Alton	104.00	130.00
911	1	-	1	-	Alton	Alton	120.00	150.00
912	1	-	-	80	Alton	Alton	220.00	275.00
913	1	-	-	40	Alton	Alton	120.00	150.00
914	1	-	1	-	Alton	Alton	400.00	500.00
915	1	-	1	-	Alton	Alton	240.00	300.00
916	1	-	1	-	Alton	Alton	200.00	250.00
917	1	-	1	-	Alton	London	360.00	450.00
918	1	-	-	80	Alton	Alton	120.00	150.00
919	1	-	-	80	Alton	Alton	200.00	250.00
920	1	-	-	80	Alton	Alton	120.00	150.00
921	1	-	-	80	Alton	Alton	184.00	230.00
922	1	-	-	80	Alton	Alton	200.00	250.00
923	1	-	-	80	Alton	Alton	200.00	250.00
924	1	-	-	80	Alton	Alton	120.00	150.00
925	1	-	-	80	Alton	Barrington	120.00	150.00
926	1	-	-	80	Alton	Alton	400.00	500.00
1001	1	-	-	40	Alton	Alton	296.00	370.00
1002	1	-	-	80	Alton	Dover	100.60	125.75
1003	1	-	-	80	Alton	Dover	200.00	250.00
1004	1	-	-	80	Alton	Dover	120.00	150.00
1005	.5	-	-	80	Alton	Alton	80.80	101.00
1006	1	-	-	80	Alton	Alton	200.00	250.00
1007	1	-	-	80	Alton	Alton	160.00	200.00
1008	1	-	-	40	Alton	Alton	120.00	150.00

1798 DIRECT TAX

Pg/No.	Occupant Surname	Occupant First Name	Owner Surname	Owner First Name	Exempt Dwg	Exempt Acr	Exempt Per
1009	Peirce	Joseph	Peirce	Joseph	-	-	-
1010	Peavey	Oliver	Peavey	Oliver	-	-	-
1011	McDuffee	Daniel	Rogers	Daniel	-	-	-
1012	Small	Joseph	Small	Joseph	-	-	-
1013	Smith	Josiah	Smith	Josiah	-	-	-
1014	Smith	Reuben	Smith	Reuben	-	-	-
1015	Stockbridge	Israel	Stockbridge	Israel	-	-	-
1016	Woodman	Jeremiah	Woodman	Jeremiah	-	-	-

NEW HAMPSHIRE   DISTRICT 13

Pg/No.	Dwg	Out Hou	Acr	Per	Property Location	Residence of Owner	Value $	Eq Val $
1009	1	–	–	80	Alton	Alton	320.00	400.00
1010	1	–	–	80	Alton	Alton	120.00	150.00
1011	.5	–	–	80	Alton	Rochester	80.80	101.00
1012	1	–	–	80	Alton	Alstead	160.00	200.00
1013	1	–	–	40	Alton	Alstead	160.00	200.00
1014	1	–	–	80	Alton	Alstead	100.60	125.75
1015	1	–	–	80	Alton	Alstead	200.00	250.00
1016	1	–	–	80	Alton	Alstead	180.00	225.00

Schedule D is signed on page 10 as follows:
    State of New Hampshire
    Exeter 12th of September, 1799
    The foregoing are the Valuations of Dwelling Houses &c as revised and equalized by us.
    (Signed) Nat. Gilman
            Joseph Badger, Jr.
            Jonathan Atherton
            John Bellows
            David Hough
        Commissioners of the State of New Hampshire

SCHEDULE E

GENERAL LIST of Lands, Lots, Buildings, and Wharves, owned, possessed or occupied on the first day of October, 1798, within the Assessment District No. 13 in the State of New Hampshire, excepting only such Dwelling-Houses as, with Out-Houses appurtenant thereto, and the lots on which they are erected, not exceeding two Acres in any case, are above the value of One Hundred Dollars.

    Page and entry number.
    Names of Occupants or Possessors.
    Names of Reputed Owners.
    Dwelling Houses and out-Houses of a value not exceeding one hundred Dollars.
        No. of Dwelling Houses.
        Value.
          Doll.
          Cents.
        Quantities of Land, Lots &c. exempted from Valuation.
          Acres.
          Perches.
          Sqr. Ft.
    Land, Lots, &c. subject to and included in the Valuation.
        Acres.
        Perches.
        Sqr. Ft
In what Township or Parish in the Assessment District situated.
Place of residence of the Reputed owners.
Valuations as determined by the Principal Assessors, including Dwelling Houses &c not exceeding one hundred dollars in value.
    Dollars
    Cents.
Rate percentum of 24 addition prescribed by the Commissioners.
1. Valuations as revised & equalized by the Commissioners.
    Dollars.
    Cents.
2. Whole Valuation of Lands belonging to or possessed by one Person.
    Dollars.
    Cents.

Editor's note: Because of space constraints, the Sqr. Ft. columns were not included in this transcription since there are no square feet values entered in the original record. The first two numbers for each line represent the page number of the schedule and the last 2 numbers represent the line number on the page

1798 DIRECT TAX

Pg/No	Occupant Surname	Occupant First Name	Owner Surname	Owner First Name	Dwg #	Val $	Expt Acr
101	Adams	Asa	Adams	Asa	1	50	-
102	Allard	Henry	Allard	Henry	-	-	-
103	Allen	Ebenezer	Allen	Ebenezer	-	-	82
104	Unimproved	-	Allen	Ebenezer	-	-	354
105	Bassett	Daniel	Bassett	Daniel	-	-	-
106	Unimproved	-	Bassett	Daniel	-	-	-
107	Bickford	Jonathan	Bickford	Jonathan	-	-	-
108	Bickford	Jonathan, Jr.	Bickford	Jonathan Jr.	1	30	-
109	Bickford	Wilmot	Bickford	Wilmot	-	-	-
110	Blake	Benj & Jonathan	Blake	Benj & Jonathan	-	-	-
111	Brackett	Benning	Brackett	Benning	1	30	-
112	Brackett	John	Brackett	John	1	5	-
113	Brewster	Daniel, Jr.	Brewster	Daniel, Jr.	1	30	-
114	Brewster	George	Brewster	George	-	-	-
115	Brown	Moses	Brown	Moses	-	-	-
116	Brown	Nathaniel	Brown	Nathaniel	-	-	-
117	Cate	James	Cate	James	1	15	-
118	Chase	Thomas	Chase	Thomas	-	-	-
119	Chamberlain	Jason	Chamberlain	Jason	-	-	-
120	Clifford	Lemuel	Clifford	Lemuel	1	1	-
121	Clemmont	Gershom	Clemmont	Gershom	1	5	-
122	Coleman	James	Coleman	James	1	10	-
201	Connor	James	Connor	James	-	-	-
202	Unimproved	-	Connor	James	-	-	-
203	Unimproved	-	Connor	James	-	-	-
204	Unimproved	-	Connor	James	-	-	-
205	Unimproved	-	Connor	James	-	-	-
206	Connor	James, Jr.	Connor	James, Jr.	1	30	-
207	Copp	David	Copp	David	-	-	-
208	Cotton	James	Cotton	James	-	-	-
209	Cotton	John	Cotton	John	1	30	-
210	Cotton	Thomas	Cotton	Thomas	-	-	-
211	Unimproved	-	Cotton	Thomas	-	-	-
212	Cotton	William	Cotton	William	-	-	-
213	Cotton	William, Jr.	Cotton	William, Jr.	1	20	-
214	Unimproved	-	Cotton	William, Jr.	-	-	-
215	Unimproved	-	Cutter	A.R.	-	-	-
216	Unimproved	-	Cutter	A.R.	-	-	-
217	Drew	Isaac	Drew	Isaac	1	40	-
218	Drew	John	Drew	John	1	18	-
219	Drew	Jedidiah	Drew	Jedidiah	-	-	-
220	Drew	Thomas	Drew	Thomas	1	15	-
221	Unimproved	-	Evans	Stephen	-	-	-
222	Estes	Samuel	Estes	Samuel	-	-	-
223	Edmunds	Jonathan	Edmunds	Jonathan	-	-	-
224	Evans	Benjamin	Evans	Benjamin	-	-	-
225	Evans	Joseph	Evans	Joseph	1	10	-

NEW HAMPSHIRE DISTRICT 13

Pg/No	Ext Per	Acr	Per	Property Location	Residence of Owner	Value $	Eq. Val $	Total $
101	-	45	-	Wolfeboro	Wolfeboro	275.00	341.00	341.00
102	-	80	-	Wolfeboro	Wolfeboro	530.00	657.20	657.20
103	-	-	-	Wolfeboro	Wolfeboro	-	-	-
104	-	-	-	Wolfeboro	Wolfeboro	-	-	-
105	-	100	-	Wolfeboro	Wolfeboro	670.00	830.80	-
106	-	51	-	Wolfeboro	Wolfeboro	100.00	124.00	954.80
107	-	100	-	Wolfeboro	Wolfeboro	640.00	793.60	793.60
108	-	100	-	Wolfeboro	Wolfeboro	500.00	620.00	620.00
109	-	80	-	Wolfeboro	Wolfeboro	264.00	327.36	327.36
110	-	99	-	Wolfeboro	Wolfeboro	725.00	899.00	899.00
111	-	-	-	Wolfeboro	Wolfeboro	40.00	49.60	49.60
112	-	80	-	Wolfeboro	Wolfeboro	360.00	446.40	446.40
113	-	200	-	Wolfeboro	Wolfeboro	780.00	967.20	967.20
114	-	150	-	Wolfeboro	Wolfeboro	585.00	725.40	725.40
115	-	100	-	Wolfeboro	Wolfeboro	470.00	582.80	582.80
116	-	203	80	Wolfeboro	Wolfeboro	1000.00	1240.00	1240.00
117	-	100	-	Wolfeboro	Wolfeboro	350.00	434.00	434.00
118	-	100	-	Wolfeboro	Wolfeboro	866.00	1073.84	1073.84
119	-	90	-	Wolfeboro	Wolfeboro	240.00	297.60	297.60
120	-	100	-	Wolfeboro	Wolfeboro	530.00	657.20	657.20
121	-	45	-	Wolfeboro	Wolfeboro	90.00	111.60	111.60
122	-	105	-	Wolfeboro	Wolfeboro	325.00	403.00	403.00
201	-	100	-	Wolfeboro	Wolfeboro	740.00	917.60	-
202	-	40	-	Wolfeboro	Wolfeboro	20.00	24.80	-
203	-	24	-	Wolfeboro	Wolfeboro	48.00	59.52	-
204	-	22	-	Wolfeboro	Wolfeboro	11.00	13.64	-
205	-	112	-	Wolfeboro	Wolfeboro	168.00	208.32	1223.88
206	-	100	-	Wolfeboro	Wolfeboro	350.00	434.00	434.00
207	-	99	80	Wolfeboro	Wolfeboro	450.00	558.00	558.00
208	-	95	-	Wolfeboro	Wolfeboro	350.00	434.00	434.00
209	-	100	-	Wolfeboro	Wolfeboro	445.00	551.80	551.80
210	-	80	-	Wolfeboro	Wolfeboro	350.00	434.00	-
211	-	50	-	Wolfeboro	Wolfeboro	75.00	93.00	527.00
212	-	100	-	Wolfeboro	Wolfeboro	540.00	669.60	669.60
213	-	-	-	Wolfeboro	Wolfeboro	110.00	136.40	-
214	-	-	-	Wolfeboro	Wolfeboro	130.00	161.20	297.60
215	-	350	-	Wolfeboro	Portsmouth	525.00	651.00	-
216	-	200	-	Wolfeboro	Portsmouth	300.00	372.00	1023.00
217	-	75	-	Wolfeboro	Wolfeboro	350.00	434.00	434.00
218	-	60	-	Wolfeboro	Wolfeboro	200.00	248.00	248.00
219	-	120	-	Wolfeboro	Wolfeboro	380.00	471.20	471.20
220	-	-	-	Wolfeboro	Wolfeboro	140.00	173.60	173.60
221	-	284	-	Wolfeboro	Dover	426.00	528.24	528.24
222	-	100	-	Wolfeboro	Wolfeboro	450.00	558.00	558.00
223	-	156	-	Wolfeboro	Wolfeboro	500.00	620.00	620.00
224	-	-	-	Wolfeboro	Wolfeboro	18.00	22.39	22.39
225	-	90	-	Wolfeboro	Wolfeboro	210.00	260.40	260.40

1798 DIRECT TAX

Pg/No	Occupant Surname	Occupant First Name	Owner Surname	Owner First Name	Dwg #	Val $	Expt Acr
226	Edmonds	John	Edmonds	John	1	80	-
301	Fernald	James	Fernald	James	-	-	-
302	Fernald	John W.	Fernald	John W.	1	30	-
303	Unimproved	-	Fernald	John W.	-	-	-
304	Fernald	William	Fernald	William	1	20	-
305	Unimproved	-	Fernald	John	-	-	-
306	Folsom	Jacob	Folsom	Jacob	1	50	-
307	Marden	James	Fox	Samuel	-	-	-
308	Frost	Aaron	Frost	Aaron	-	-	-
309	Frost	Aaron, Jr.	Frost	Aaron, Jr.	-	-	-
310	Frost	Josiah	Frost	Josiah	1	30	-
311	Fullerton	James	Fullerton	James	-	-	-
312	Fullerton	John	Fullerton	John	-	-	-
313	Unimproved	-	Fullerton	John	-	-	-
314	Fullerton	William	Fullerton	William	1	20	-
315	Furber	John	Furber	John	-	-	-
316	Unimproved	-	Gore	Francis	-	-	-
317	-	-	Grover	Samuel	-	-	-
318	Glover	Richard	Glover	Richard	-	-	-
319	Goldsmith	Isaac	Goldsmith	Isaac	1	30	-
320	Guppy	William	Guppy	William	1	10	-
321	Unimproved	-	Glyn	George	-	-	-
322	Unimproved	-	Hodgdon	Caleb	-	-	-
323	Hardy	Dudley	Hardy	Dudley	-	-	-
324	Hains	Jacob	Hains	Jacob	-	-	-
325	Hains	Joseph	Hains	Joseph	-	-	-
326	Hains	Joshua	Hains	Joshua	-	-	-
327	Unimproved	-	Hersey	James	-	-	-
401	Hersey	Jonathan	Hersey	Jonathan	-	-	-
402	Unimproved	-	Hersey	Jonathan	-	-	-
403	Hersey	Samuel	Hersey	Samuel	-	-	-
404	Hide	Samuel	Hide	Samuel	-	-	-
405	Unimproved	-	Hide	Samuel	-	-	-
406	Hide	Stephen	Hide	Stephen	-	-	-
407	Hodgdon	Theodore	Hodgdon	Theodore	1	10	-
408	Horn	Benjamin	Horn	Benjamin	-	-	-
409	Unimproved	-	Horn	Benjamin	-	-	-
410	Horn	Ebenezar, Jr.	Horn	Ebenezar, Jr	1	40	-
411	Horn	Isaiah	Horn	Isaiah	-	-	-
412	Unimproved	-	Horn	Isaiah	-	-	-
413	Horn	John	Horn	John	-	-	-
414	Horn	Stephen	Horn	Stephen	-	-	-
415	Unimproved	-	Horn	Stephen	-	-	-
416	Unimproved	-	Jaffrey	George	-	-	-
417	Jewett	Andrew	Jewett	Andrew	-	-	-
418	Jenness	Cornelius	Jenness	Cornelius	1	6	-
419	Judkins	John	Judkins	John	1	20	-

NEW HAMPSHIRE DISTRICT 13

Pg/No	Ext Per	Acr	Per	Property Location	Residence of Owner	Value $	Eq. Val $	Total $
226	-	200	-	Wolfeboro	Wolfeboro	900.00	1116.00	1116.00
301	-	450	-	Wolfeboro	Wolfeboro	1700.00	2108.00	2108.00
302	-	50	-	Wolfeboro	Wolfeboro	270.00	334.80	-
303	-	25	-	Wolfeboro	Wolfeboro	60.00	74.40	409.20
304	-	50	-	Wolfeboro	Wolfeboro	220.00	272.80	272.80
305	-	50	-	Wolfeboro	Brookfield	100.00	124.00	124.00
306	-	80	-	Wolfeboro	Wolfeboro	400.00	496.00	496.00
307	-	85	-	Wolfeboro	Louden	330.00	409.20	409.20
308	-	150	-	Wolfeboro	Wolfeboro	650.00	806.00	806.00
309	-	90	-	Wolfeboro	Wolfeboro	270.00	334.80	334.80
310	-	100	-	Wolfeboro	Wolfeboro	280.00	347.20	347.20
311	-	100	-	Wolfeboro	Wolfeboro	680.00	843.20	843.20
312	-	100	-	Wolfeboro	Wolfeboro	600.00	744.00	-
313	-	50	-	Wolfeboro	Wolfeboro	75.00	93.00	837.00
314	-	120	-	Wolfeboro	Wolfeboro	500.00	620.00	620.00
315	-	139	-	Wolfeboro	Wolfeboro	730.00	905.20	905.20
316	-	-	-	Wolfeboro	Unknown	100.00	124.00	124.00
317	-	120	-	Wolfeboro	Wolfeboro	180.00	223.20	223.20
318	-	28	-	Wolfeboro	Wolfeboro	30.00	37.20	37.20
319	-	100	-	Wolfeboro	Wolfeboro	650.00	806.00	806.00
320	-	100	-	Wolfeboro	Wolfeboro	510.00	632.40	632.40
321	-	150	-	Wolfeboro	Unknown	215.00	266.60	266.60
322	-	300	-	Wolfeboro	Dover	450.00	558.00	558.00
323	-	119	-	Wolfeboro	Wolfeboro	630.00	781.20	781.20
324	-	75	-	Wolfeboro	Wolfeboro	330.00	409.20	409.20
325	-	75	-	Wolfeboro	Wolfeboro	340.00	421.60	421.60
326	-	150	-	Wolfeboro	Wolfeboro	900.00	1116.00	1116.00
327	-	68	-	Wolfeboro	Wolfeboro	100.00	124.00	124.00
401	-	200	-	Wolfeboro	Wolfeboro	1250.00	1550.00	-
402	-	25	-	Wolfeboro	Wolfeboro	40.00	49.60	1599.60
403	-	80	-	Wolfeboro	Wolfeboro	120.00	148.80	148.80
404	-	50	-	Wolfeboro	Wolfeboro	320.00	396.80	-
405	-	50	-	Wolfeboro	Wolfeboro	100.00	124.00	520.80
406	-	50	-	Wolfeboro	Wolfeboro	100.00	124.00	124.00
407	-	74	-	Wolfeboro	Wolfeboro	158.00	195.92	195.92
408	-	75	-	Wolfeboro	Wolfeboro	550.00	682.00	-
409	-	40	-	Wolfeboro	Wolfeboro	120.00	148.80	830.80
410	-	70	-	Wolfeboro	Wolfeboro	400.00	496.00	496.00
411	-	80	-	Wolfeboro	Wolfeboro	655.00	812.20	-
412	-	50	-	Wolfeboro	Wolfeboro	150.00	186.00	998.20
413	-	70	-	Wolfeboro	Wolfeboro	500.00	620.00	620.00
414	-	89	80	Wolfeboro	Wolfeboro	650.00	806.00	-
415	-	50	-	Wolfeboro	Wolfeboro	150.00	186.00	992.00
416	-	120	-	Wolfeboro	Portsmouth	360.00	446.40	446.40
417	-	-	120	Wolfeboro	Wolfeboro	42.00	52.08	52.08
418	-	60	-	Wolfeboro	Wolfeboro	280.00	347.20	347.20
419	-	3	-	Wolfeboro	Wolfeboro	35.00	43.40	43.40

1798 DIRECT TAX

Pg/No	Occupant Surname	Occupant First Name	Owner Surname	Owner First Name	Dwg #	Val $	Expt Acr
420	-	-	Johnson	Phinehas	-	-	-
421	Jones	Isaac	Jones	Isaac	-	-	-
422	Key	Love	Key	Love	1	10	-
423	Kennison	Joseph	Kennison	Joseph	-	-	-
424	Brown	Nathaniel	Lane	George	-	-	-
425	Unimproved	-	Lane	George	-	-	-
426	Leavitt	Edward	Leavitt	Edward	1	20	-
501	Lary	John	Lary	John	-	-	-
502	Unimproved	-	Lear	William	-	-	-
503	Leavitt	Samuel	Leavitt	Samuel	1	20	-
504	Libby	Reuben	Libby	Reuben	-	-	-
505	Wille	Samuel	Libby	Reuben	1	25	-
506	Unimproved	-	Libby	Reuben	-	-	-
507	Unimproved	-	Libby	Reuben	-	-	-
508	Unimproved	-	Libby	Reuben	-	-	-
509	Lucas	Andrew	Lucas	Andrew	1	80	-
510	Lucas	James	Lucas	James	1	40	-
511	Lucas	James	Lucas	James	-	-	-
512	Unimproved	-	Lucas	James	-	-	-
513	Lucas	John	Lucas	John	1	20	-
514	Lucas	Nehemiah	Lucas	Nehemiah	-	-	-
515	Unimproved	-	Public Lands	-	-	-	300
516	Unimproved	-	Public Lands	-	-	-	10
517	Unimproved	-	Public Lands	-	-	-	51
518	Mardin	James, Jr	Mardin	James, Jr	-	-	-
519	Mardin	James, Jr	Mardin	James, Jr	-	-	-
520	Martin	Isaac	Martin	Isaac	-	-	-
521	Unimproved	-	Martin	Thomas	-	-	-
522	Meder	Ebenezer	Meder	Ebenezer	-	-	-
523	Unimproved	-	Meder	Ebenezer	-	-	-
524	Moody	Abner	Moody	Abner	-	-	-
525	Unimproved	-	Nud	Benjamin, Jr.	-	-	-
526	-	-	Neal	Joshua	-	-	-
601	Norris	Jeremiah	Norris	Jeremiah	1	50	-
602	Gould	Jeremiah	Nowell	Samuel	-	-	-
603	Nudd	Samuel	Nudd	Samuel	1	40	-
604	Nudd	William	Nudd	William	1	40	-
605	Nute	Thomas	Nute	Thomas	1	30	-
606	Nutt	Samuel	Nutt	Samuel	1	20	-
607	Nute	James, Jr.	Nute	James, Jr.	-	-	-
608	Piper	David	Piper	David	1	70	-
609	Piper	John	Piper	John	-	-	-
610	Perkins	Thomas	Perkins	Thomas	-	-	-
611	Unimproved	-	Peirce	John	-	-	-
612	Unimproved	-	Penhollow	John	-	-	-
613	Unimproved	-	Reed	Michael	-	-	-
614	Rogers	William	Rogers	William	-	-	-

NEW HAMPSHIRE DISTRICT 13

Pg/No	Ext Per	Acr	Per	Property Location	Residence of Owner	Value $	Eq. Val $	Total $
420	-	100	-	Wolfeboro	Brookfield	300.00	372.00	372.00
421	-	25	-	Wolfeboro	Alton	100.00	124.00	124.00
422	-	63	-	Wolfeboro	Wolfeboro	160.00	198.40	198.40
423	-	50	-	Wolfeboro	Wolfeboro	340.00	421.60	421.60
424	-	1918	-	Wolfeboro	Charleston MA	10077.00	12495.48	-
425	-	400	-	Wolfeboro	Charleston MA	800.00	992.00	13487.48
426	-	71	-	Wolfeboro	Wolfeboro	300.00	372.00	372.00
501	-	65	-	Wolfeboro	Wolfeboro	200.00	248.00	248.00
502	-	50	-	Wolfeboro	Wolfeboro	100.00	124.00	124.00
503	-	100	-	Wolfeboro	Wolfeboro	700.00	868.00	868.00
504	-	5	80	Wolfeboro	Wolfeboro	50.00	62.00	-
505	-	105	-	Wolfeboro	Wolfeboro	700.00	868.00	-
506	-	50	-	Wolfeboro	Wolfeboro	100.00	124.00	-
507	-	75	-	Wolfeboro	Wolfeboro	200.00	248.00	-
508	-	50	-	Wolfeboro	Wolfeboro	100.00	124.00	1426.00
509	-	99	80	Wolfeboro	Wolfeboro	670.00	830.80	830.80
510	-	87	-	Wolfeboro	Wolfeboro	390.00	483.60	-
511	-	60	-	Wolfeboro	Wolfeboro	180.00	223.20	-
512	-	60	-	Wolfeboro	Wolfeboro	180.00	223.20	930.00
513	-	106	-	Wolfeboro	Wolfeboro	320.00	396.80	396.80
514	-	58	-	Wolfeboro	Wolfeboro	150.00	186.00	186.00
515	-	-	-	Wolfeboro	Wolfeboro	-	-	-
516	-	-	-	Wolfeboro	Wolfeboro	-	-	-
517	-	-	-	Wolfeboro	Wolfeboro	-	-	-
518	-	49	-	Wolfeboro	Wolfeboro	147.00	182.28	-
519	-	51	-	Wolfeboro	Wolfeboro	153.00	189.72	372.00
520	-	100	-	Wolfeboro	Wolfeboro	530.00	657.20	657.20
521	-	104	-	Wolfeboro	Portsmouth	104.00	128.96	128.96
522	-	99	80	Wolfeboro	Wolfeboro	650.00	806.00	-
523	-	12	-	Wolfeboro	Wolfeboro	50.00	62.00	868.00
524	-	50	-	Wolfeboro	Ossipee	175.00	217.00	217.00
525	-	50	-	Wolfeboro	Greenland	150.00	186.00	186.00
526	-	100	-	Wolfeboro	Wolfeboro	250.00	310.00	310.00
601	-	3	-	Wolfeboro	Wolfeboro	88.00	109.12	109.12
602	-	50	-	Wolfeboro	Lynn, MA	200.00	248.00	248.00
603	-	50	-	Wolfeboro	Wolfeboro	250.00	310.00	310.00
604	-	50	-	Wolfeboro	Wolfeboro	220.00	272.80	272.80
605	-	62	80	Wolfeboro	Wolfeboro	330.00	409.20	409.20
606	-	50	-	Wolfeboro	Wolfeboro	145.00	179.80	179.80
607	-	190	-	Wolfeboro	Wolfeboro	285.00	353.40	353.40
608	-	78	-	Wolfeboro	Wolfeboro	300.00	372.00	372.00
609	-	40	-	Wolfeboro	Wolfeboro	130.00	161.20	161.20
610	-	50	-	Wolfeboro	Ossipee	150.00	186.00	186.00
611	-	478	-	Wolfeboro	Portsmouth	1000.00	1240.00	1240.00
612	-	200	-	Wolfeboro	Portsmouth	200.00	248.00	248.00
613	-	300	-	Wolfeboro	Dover	450.00	558.00	558.00
614	-	99	80	Wolfeboro	Wolfeboro	750.00	930.00	-

1798 DIRECT TAX

Pg/No	Occupant Surname	Occupant First Name	Owner Surname	Owner First Name	Dwg #	Val $	Expt Acr
615	Unimproved	-	Rogers	William	-	-	-
616	Unimproved	-	Rogers	William	-	-	-
617	Unimproved	-	Rogers	William	-	-	-
618	Unimproved	-	Rogers	William	-	-	-
619	Rust	Henry	Rust	Henry	-	-	-
620	Rust	Henry, Jr.	Rust	Henry, Jr.	-	-	-
621	Rust	Richard	Rust	Richard	-	-	-
622	Unimproved	-	Rindge	Daniel	-	-	-
623	Unimproved	-	Rindge	Daniel	-	-	-
624	Seavey	Moses	Seavey	Moses	1	30	-
625	Smith	Jacob	Smith	Jacob	-	-	-
626	Snell	John	Snell	John	-	-	-
701	Shorey	John	Shorey	John	-	-	-
702	Shortridge	John	Shortridge	John	-	-	-
703	Swasey	John	Swasey	John	1	30	-
704	Unimproved	-	Suthern	James	-	-	-
705	Unimproved	-	Sheafe	James	-	-	-
706	Unimproved	-	Sheafe	James	-	-	-
707	Unimproved	-	Sheafe	James	-	-	-
708	Unimproved	-	Sheafe	James	-	-	-
709	Unimproved	-	Sheafe	James	-	-	-
710	Swasey	Thomas	Swasey	Thomas	1	20	-
711	Unimproved	-	Serjeant	Nathaniel Heirs	-	-	-
712	Tibbets	Ebenezer	Tibbets	Ebenezer	1	28	-
713	Tibbets	Ichabod	Tibbets	Ichabod	-	-	-
714	Tibbets	Jonathan	Tibbets	Jonathan	1	10	-
715	Tibbets	Levi & Benj.	Tibbets	Levi & Benj.	-	-	-
716	Tibbets	Richard	Tibbets	Richard	-	-	-
717	Tibbets	Samuel	Tibbets	Samuel	1	80	-
718	Thurston	Moses	Thurston	Moses	-	-	-
719	Townsend	Isaac	Townsend	Isaac	-	-	-
720	Thurston	Josiah	Thurston	Josiah	1	42	-
721	Trask	Hannah	Trask	Hannah	-	-	-
722	Unimproved	-	Treadwell	Robert C.	-	-	-
723	Triggs	William	Triggs	William	-	-	-
724	Unimproved	-	Triggs	William	-	-	-
725	Unimproved	-	Tucker	Samuel	-	-	-
726	Unimproved	-	Unknown	-	-	-	-
801	Unimproved	-	Unknown	-	-	-	-
802	Unimproved	-	Unknown	-	-	-	-
803	Unimproved	-	Unknown	-	-	-	-
804	Unimproved	-	Unknown	-	-	-	-
805	Unimproved	-	Unknown	-	-	-	-
806	Unimproved	-	Unknown	-	-	-	-
807	Unimproved	-	Unknown	-	-	-	-
808	Unimproved	-	Unknown	-	-	-	-
809	Varney	Joseph	Varney	Joseph	-	-	-

NEW HAMPSHIRE DISTRICT 13

Pg/No	Ext Per	Acr	Per	Property Location	Residence of Owner	Value $	Eq. Val $	Total $
615	-	120	-	Wolfeboro	Wolfeboro	360.00	446.40	-
616	-	50	-	Wolfeboro	Wolfeboro	75.00	93.00	-
617	-	49	80	Wolfeboro	Wolfeboro	75.00	93.00	-
618	-	50	-	Wolfeboro	Wolfeboro	75.00	93.00	1655.40
619	-	320	-	Wolfeboro	Wolfeboro	1150.00	1426.00	1426.00
620	-	202	-	Wolfeboro	Wolfeboro	750.00	930.00	930.00
621	-	130	-	Wolfeboro	Wolfeboro	660.00	818.40	818.40
622	-	128	-	Wolfeboro	Portsmouth	200.00	248.00	-
623	-	200	-	Wolfeboro	Portsmouth	200.00	248.00	496.00
624	-	50	-	Wolfeboro	Wolfeboro	200.00	248.00	248.00
625	-	95	-	Wolfeboro	Wolfeboro	530.00	657.20	657.20
626	-	45	-	Wolfeboro	Wolfeboro	135.00	167.40	167.40
701	-	50	-	Wolfeboro	Wolfeboro	150.00	186.00	186.00
702	-	20	-	Wolfeboro	Wolfeboro	60.00	74.40	74.40
703	-	70	-	Wolfeboro	Wolfeboro	330.00	409.20	409.20
704	-	50	-	Wolfeboro	Wolfeboro	100.00	124.00	124.00
705	-	335	-	Wolfeboro	Portsmouth	500.00	620.00	-
706	-	480	-	Wolfeboro	Portsmouth	960.00	1190.40	-
707	-	100	-	Wolfeboro	Portsmouth	200.00	248.00	-
708	-	100	-	Wolfeboro	Portsmouth	200.00	248.00	-
709	-	52	-	Wolfeboro	Portsmouth	104.00	128.96	2435.36
710	-	30	-	Wolfeboro	Exeter	120.00	148.80	148.80
711	-	182	-	Wolfeboro	Wolfeboro	250.00	310.00	310.00
712	-	50	-	Wolfeboro	Wolfeboro	260.00	322.40	322.40
713	-	50	-	Wolfeboro	Wolfeboro	200.00	248.00	248.00
714	-	100	-	Wolfeboro	Wolfeboro	326.00	404.24	404.24
715	-	99	80	Wolfeboro	Wolfeboro	600.00	744.00	744.00
716	-	50	-	Wolfeboro	Wolfeboro	125.00	155.00	155.00
717	-	100	-	Wolfeboro	Wolfeboro	614.00	761.36	761.36
718	-	49	80	Wolfeboro	Wolfeboro	200.00	248.00	248.00
719	-	88	-	Wolfeboro	Wolfeboro	400.00	496.00	496.00
720	-	-	80	Wolfeboro	Wolfeboro	50.00	62.00	62.00
721	-	200	-	Wolfeboro	Wolfeboro	845.00	1047.80	1047.80
722	-	100	-	Wolfeboro	Portsmouth	100.00	124.00	124.00
723	-	80	-	Wolfeboro	Wolfeboro	350.00	434.00	-
724	-	51	-	Wolfeboro	Wolfeboro	125.00	155.00	589.00
725	-	72	-	Wolfeboro	Portsmouth	108.00	133.92	133.92
726	-	100	-	Wolfeboro	Wolfeboro	175.00	217.00	217.00
801	-	300	-	Wolfeboro	Wolfeboro	600.00	744.00	744.00
802	-	300	-	Wolfeboro	Wolfeboro	600.00	744.00	744.00
803	-	300	-	Wolfeboro	Wolfeboro	450.00	558.00	558.00
804	-	300	-	Wolfeboro	Wolfeboro	600.00	744.00	744.00
805	-	200	-	Wolfeboro	Wolfeboro	400.00	496.00	496.00
806	-	50	-	Wolfeboro	Wolfeboro	25.00	31.00	31.00
807	-	300	-	Wolfeboro	Wolfeboro	450.00	558.00	558.00
808	-	200	-	Wolfeboro	Wolfeboro	300.00	372.00	372.00
809	-	112	-	Wolfeboro	Wolfeboro	650.00	806.00	-

1798 DIRECT TAX

Pg/No	Occupant Surname	Occupant First Name	Owner Surname	Owner First Name	Dwg #	Val $	Expt Acr
810	Unimproved	-	Varney	Joseph	-	-	-
811	Warren	George	Warren	George	-	-	-
812	Warren	John	Warren	John	-	-	-
813	Wentworth	Daniel	Wentworth	Daniel	1	30	-
814	Whitten	Jesse	Whitten	Jesse	1	60	-
815	Whittle	Thomas	Whittle	Thomas	-	-	-
816	Wille	Josiah	Wille	Josiah	1	10	-
817	Wiggin	Andrew	Wiggin	Andrew	-	-	-
818	Wiggin	Andrew, Jr	Wiggin	Andrew, Jr.	1	40	-
819	Wiggin	Daniel	Wiggin	Daniel	1	10	-
820	Wiggin	Joshua	Wiggin	Joshua	-	-	-
821	Unimproved	-	Wiggin	Joshua	-	-	-
822	Wiggin	Mark	Wiggin	Mark	1	30	-
823	Wiggin	Paul	Wiggin	Paul	-	-	-
824	Wiggin	Rufus	Wiggin	Rufus	1	10	-
825	Wiggin	Thomas B.	Wiggin	Thomas B.	1	80	-
826	Smith	Ephraim	Wormwood	Joseph	1	20	-
901	Yeaton	George	Yeaton	George	-	-	-
902	Young	John	Young	John	-	-	-
903	Young	Thomas	Young	Thomas	1	15	-
904	Young	Zachariah	Young	Zachariah	-	-	-
905	Abbott	Elisha	Abbott	Elisha	1	25	-
906	Abbott	Samuel	Abbott	Samuel	1	26	-
907	Allard	Shadrach	Allard	Shadrach	-	-	-
908	Bickford	Aaron	Bickford	Aaron	-	-	-
909	Bickford	Nathaniel	Bickford	Nathaniel	-	-	-
910	Been	Benjamin	Been	Benjamin	1	20	-
911	Brown	Gardner	Brown	Gardner	-	-	-
912	Brown	John	Brown	John	-	-	-
913	Brown	John	Brown	John	-	-	-
914	Brown	John	Brown	John	-	-	-
915	Brown	John	Brown	John	-	-	-
916	Brown	John	Brown	John	-	-	-
917	Brown	Jonathan	Brown	Jonathan	1	25	-
918	Brown	Moores	Brown	Moores	1	15	-
919	Brown	Stephen	Brown	Stephen	1	20	-
920	Burbank	Jonathan	Burbank	Jonathan	-	-	-
921	Canney	Benjamin	Canney	Benjamin	-	-	-
922	Canney	Benjamin, Jr.	Canney	Benjamin, Jr.	-	-	-
923	Canney	Benjamin	Canney	Benjamin	-	-	-
924	Canney	Joseph	Canney	Joseph	-	-	-
925	Unimproved	-	Canney	Edmund & Joseph	-	-	-
926	Copp	William	Copp	William	-	-	-
1001	Canney	William	Canney	William	-	-	-
1002	-	-	Copp	Tristram	-	-	-
1003	Copp	Tristram, Jr.	Copp	Tristram, Jr.	1	30	-
1004	Copp	Moses	Copp	Moses	-	-	-

NEW HAMPSHIRE DISTRICT 13

Pg/No	Ext Per	Acr	Per	Property Location	Residence of Owner	Value $	Eq. Val $	Total $
810	-	51	-	Wolfeboro	Wolfeboro	102.00	126.48	932.48
811	-	136	-	Wolfeboro	Wolfeboro	600.00	744.00	744.00
812	-	37	-	Wolfeboro	Wolfeboro	111.00	137.64	137.64
813	-	70	-	Wolfeboro	Wolfeboro	200.00	248.00	248.00
814	-	69	-	Wolfeboro	Wolfeboro	350.00	434.00	434.00
815	-	50	-	Wolfeboro	Wolfeboro	400.00	496.00	496.00
816	-	49	-	Wolfeboro	Wolfeboro	130.00	161.20	161.20
817	-	100	-	Wolfeboro	Wolfeboro	500.00	620.00	620.00
818	-	18	120	Wolfeboro	Wolfeboro	130.00	161.20	161.20
819	-	100	-	Wolfeboro	Wolfeboro	600.00	744.00	744.00
820	-	90	-	Wolfeboro	Wolfeboro	294.00	364.56	-
821	-	51	-	Wolfeboro	Wolfeboro	102.00	126.48	491.04
822	-	20	-	Wolfeboro	Wolfeboro	130.00	161.20	161.20
823	-	75	-	Wolfeboro	Wolfeboro	280.00	347.20	347.20
824	-	105	-	Wolfeboro	Wolfeboro	325.00	403.00	403.00
825	-	50	-	Wolfeboro	Wolfeboro	330.00	409.20	409.20
826	-	100	-	Wolfeboro	Durham	400.00	496.00	496.00
901	-	100	-	Wolfeboro	Wolfeboro	250.00	310.00	310.00
902	-	300	-	Wolfeboro	Wolfeboro	1200.00	1488.00	1488.00
903	-	50	-	Wolfeboro	Wolfeboro	140.00	173.60	173.60
904	-	50	-	Wolfeboro	Wolfeboro	220.00	272.80	-
905	-	100	-	Tuftonboro	Tuftonboro	200.00	248.00	248.00
906	-	100	-	Tuftonboro	Tuftonboro	400.00	496.00	496.00
907	-	50	-	Tuftonboro	Tuftonboro	150.00	186.00	186.00
908	-	68	-	Tuftonboro	Tuftonboro	200.00	248.00	248.00
909	-	100	-	Tuftonboro	Tuftonboro	300.00	372.00	372.00
910	-	100	-	Tuftonboro	Tuftonboro	400.00	496.00	496.00
911	-	40	-	Tuftonboro	Tuftonboro	140.00	173.60	173.60
912	-	50	-	Tuftonboro	Tuftonboro	150.00	186.00	-
913	-	50	-	Tuftonboro	Tuftonboro	70.00	86.80	-
914	-	50	-	Tuftonboro	Tuftonboro	70.00	86.80	-
915	-	50	-	Tuftonboro	Tuftonboro	70.00	86.80	-
916	-	9	-	Tuftonboro	Tuftonboro	12.00	14.88	461.28
917	-	50	-	Tuftonboro	Tuftonboro	250.00	310.00	310.00
918	-	50	-	Tuftonboro	Tuftonboro	95.00	117.80	117.80
919	-	40	-	Tuftonboro	Tuftonboro	160.00	198.40	198.40
920	-	100	-	Tuftonboro	Tuftonboro	300.00	372.00	372.00
921	-	100	-	Tuftonboro	Tuftonboro	300.00	372.00	372.00
922	-	50	-	Tuftonboro	Tuftonboro	150.00	186.00	186.00
923	-	50	-	Tuftonboro	Tuftonboro	150.00	186.00	186.00
924	-	50	-	Tuftonboro	Tuftonboro	150.00	186.00	186.00
925	-	100	-	Tuftonboro	Somersworth	300.00	372.00	372.00
926	-	107	-	Tuftonboro	Tuftonboro	530.00	657.20	657.20
1001	-	75	-	Tuftonboro	Tuftonboro	225.00	279.00	279.00
1002	-	92	-	Tuftonboro	Rochester	276.00	342.24	342.24
1003	-	100	-	Tuftonboro	Tuftonboro	340.00	421.60	421.60
1004	-	50	-	Tuftonboro	Tuftonboro	70.00	86.80	-

1798 DIRECT TAX

Pg/No	Occupant Surname	Occupant First Name	Owner Surname	Owner First Name	Dwg #	Val $	Expt Acr
1005	Copp	Moses	Copp	Moses	-	-	-
1006	Copp	Moses	Copp	Moses	-	-	-
1007	Copp	Moses	Copp	Moses	-	-	-
1008	Copp	Moses	Copp	Moses	-	-	-
1009	Copp	Moses	Copp	Moses	-	-	-
1010	Dearborn	Joseph	Dearborn	Joseph	-	-	-
1011	-	-	Dame, Jr.	Richard	-	-	-
1012	Unimproved	-	Emery	Noah	-	-	-
1013	Unimproved	-	Emery	Noah	-	-	-
1014	Unimproved	-	Emery	Noah	-	-	-
1015	Unimproved	-	Emery	Noah	-	-	-
1016	Unimproved	-	Emery	Noah	-	-	-
1017	Unimproved	-	Emery	Noah	-	-	-
1018	Unimproved	-	Emery	Noah	-	-	-
1019	Unimproved	-	Emery	Noah	-	-	-
1020	Unimproved	-	Emery	Noah	-	-	-
1021	Unimproved	-	Emery	Noah	-	-	-
1022	Unimproved	-	Evans	Richard	-	-	-
1023	Unimproved	-	Evans	Richard	-	-	-
1024	French	James	French	James	1	15	-
1025	Graves	Phinehas	Graves	Phinehas	-	-	-
1026	-	-	Goldthwait	-	-	-	-
1101	Unimproved	-	Goddard	John	-	-	-
1102	Unimproved	-	Goddard	John	-	-	-
1103	Unimproved	-	Goddard	John	-	-	-
1104	Hall	John	Hall	John	1	30	-
1105	Hall	John	Hall	Joshua	-	-	-
1106	Hanson	Nathan	Hanson	Nathan	-	-	-
1107	Haley	William	Haley	William	1	20	-
1108	Willy	William	Horne	John	1	20	-
1109	Foss	Hinkson	Horne	Benjamin	1	20	-
1110	Horne	Ichabod	Horne	Ichabod	-	-	-
1111	Unimproved	-	Hodgdon	Jacob	-	-	-
1112	Unimproved	-	Hodgdon	Benjamin	-	-	-
1113	Unimproved	-	Holmes	Christopher	-	-	-
1114	Unimproved	-	Hodgdon	William	-	-	-
1115	Unimproved	-	Haven	Joseph	-	-	-
1116	Unimproved	-	Haven	Joseph	-	-	-
1117	Unimproved	-	Haven	Joseph	-	-	-
1118	Unimproved	-	Haven	Joseph	-	-	-
1119	Unimproved	-	Haven	John	-	-	-
1120	Unimproved	-	Haven	John	-	-	-
1121	Unimproved	-	Haven	Nathaniel A.	-	-	-
1122	Unimproved	-	Haven	Nathaniel A.	-	-	-
1123	Unimproved	-	Haven	Nathaniel A.	-	-	-
1124	Unimproved	-	Haven	Nathaniel A.	-	-	-
1125	Unimproved	-	Haven	Nathaniel A.	-	-	-

NEW HAMPSHIRE DISTRICT 13

Pg/No	Ext Per	Acr	Per	Property Location	Residence of Owner	Value $	Eq. Val $	Total $
1005	-	50	-	Tuftonboro	Tuftonboro	150.00	186.00	-
1006	-	50	-	Tuftonboro	Tuftonboro	70.00	86.80	-
1007	-	50	-	Tuftonboro	Tuftonboro	70.00	86.80	-
1008	-	9	-	Tuftonboro	Tuftonboro	12.00	14.88	-
1009	-	100	-	Tuftonboro	Tuftonboro	300.00	372.00	833.28
1010	-	95	-	Tuftonboro	Tuftonboro	510.00	632.40	632.40
1011	-	100	-	Tuftonboro	Rochester	300.00	372.00	372.00
1012	-	100	-	Tuftonboro	Exeter	150.00	186.00	-
1013	-	100	-	Tuftonboro	Tuftonboro	200.00	248.00	-
1014	-	100	-	Tuftonboro	Tuftonboro	100.00	124.00	-
1015	-	100	-	Tuftonboro	Tuftonboro	300.00	372.00	-
1016	-	100	-	Tuftonboro	Tuftonboro	300.00	372.00	-
1017	-	100	-	Tuftonboro	Tuftonboro	50.00	62.00	-
1018	-	100	-	Tuftonboro	Tuftonboro	50.00	62.00	-
1019	-	100	-	Tuftonboro	Tuftonboro	50.00	62.00	-
1020	-	100	-	Tuftonboro	Tuftonboro	50.00	62.00	-
1021	-	100	-	Tuftonboro	Tuftonboro	50.00	62.00	1612.00
1022	-	100	-	Tuftonboro	Portsmouth	175.00	217.00	-
1023	-	50	-	Tuftonboro	Tuftonboro	50.00	62.00	279.00
1024	-	25	-	Tuftonboro	Tuftonboro	130.00	161.20	161.20
1025	-	89	-	Tuftonboro	Tuftonboro	455.00	564.20	564.20
1026	-	100	-	Tuftonboro	Tuftonboro	200.00	248.00	248.00
1101	-	100	-	Tuftonboro	Portsmouth	50.00	62.00	-
1102	-	100	-	Tuftonboro	Tuftonboro	50.00	62.00	-
1103	-	49	-	Tuftonboro	Tuftonboro	100.00	124.00	248.00
1104	-	35	-	Tuftonboro	Tuftonboro	200.00	248.00	248.00
1105	-	15	-	Tuftonboro	Chester	60.00	74.40	74.40
1106	-	86	-	Tuftonboro	Tuftonboro	172.00	213.28	213.28
1107	-	47	-	Tuftonboro	Tuftonboro	150.00	186.00	186.00
1108	-	50	-	Tuftonboro	Wolfeboro	254.00	314.96	314.96
1109	-	100	-	Tuftonboro	Wolfeboro	440.00	545.60	545.60
1110	-	50	-	Tuftonboro	Tuftonboro	150.00	186.00	186.00
1111	-	50	-	Tuftonboro	Moultonboro	75.00	93.00	93.00
1112	-	100	-	Tuftonboro	Rochester	300.00	372.00	372.00
1113	-	100	-	Tuftonboro	Merredith	225.00	279.00	279.00
1114	-	50	-	Tuftonboro	Tuftonboro	50.00	62.00	62.00
1115	-	100	-	Tuftonboro	Portsmouth	100.00	124.00	-
1116	-	100	-	Tuftonboro	Tuftonboro	150.00	186.00	-
1117	-	50	-	Tuftonboro	Tuftonboro	50.00	62.00	-
1118	-	34	-	Tuftonboro	Tuftonboro	34.00	42.16	414.16
1119	-	100	-	Tuftonboro	Portsmouth	200.00	248.00	-
1120	-	100	-	Tuftonboro	Tuftonboro	200.00	248.00	496.00
1121	-	1000	-	Tuftonboro	Portsmouth	500.00	620.00	-
1122	-	80	-	Tuftonboro	Tuftonboro	40.00	49.60	-
1123	-	100	-	Tuftonboro	Tuftonboro	150.00	186.00	-
1124	-	100	-	Tuftonboro	Tuftonboro	150.00	186.00	-
1125	-	100	-	Tuftonboro	Tuftonboro	150.00	186.00	-

1798 DIRECT TAX

Pg/No	Occupant Surname	Occupant First Name	Owner Surname	Owner First Name	Dwg #	Val $	Expt Acr
1126	Unimproved	-	Haven	Nathaniel A.	-	-	-
1201	Unimproved	-	Haven	Nathaniel A.	-	-	-
1202	Unimproved	-	Haven	Nathaniel A.	-	-	-
1203	Unimproved	-	Haven	Nathaniel A.	-	-	-
1204	Unimproved	-	Haven	Nathaniel A.	-	-	-
1205	Unimproved	-	Haven	Nathaniel A.	-	-	-
1206	Unimproved	-	Haven	Nathaniel A.	-	-	-
1207	Unimproved	-	Haven	Nathaniel A.	-	-	-
1208	Unimproved	-	Haven	Nathaniel A.	-	-	-
1209	Unimproved	-	Haven	Nathaniel A.	-	-	-
1210	Unimproved	-	Haven	Nathaniel A.	-	-	-
1211	Unimproved	-	Haven	Nathaniel A.	-	-	-
1212	-	-	Kennison	Waldron	-	-	-
1213	Lee	Ebenezar	Lee	Ebenezer	1	5	-
1214	Libbey	Hanson	Libbey	Hanson	-	-	-
1215	Leavitt	Josiah	Leavitt	Josiah	1	50	-
1216	Libby	Ichabod	Libby	Ichabod	1	30	-
1217	Unimproved	-	Langdon	Heirs of John	-	-	-
1218	Unimproved	-	Langdon	Woodbury	-	-	-
1219	Unimproved	-	Langdon	Woodbury	-	-	-
1220	Unimproved	-	Langdon	Woodbury	-	-	-
1221	Unimproved	-	Langdon	Woodbury	-	-	-
1222	Unimproved	-	Langdon	Woodbury	-	-	-
1223	Unimproved	-	Langdon	Woodbury	-	-	-
1224	Unimproved	-	Langdon	Woodbury	-	-	-
1225	Unimproved	-	Langdon	Woodbury	-	-	-
1226	Unimproved	-	Langdon	Woodbury	-	-	-
1301	Unimproved	-	Langdon	Woodbury	-	-	-
1302	Unimproved	-	Langdon	Woodbury	-	-	-
1303	Unimproved	-	Langdon	Woodbury	-	-	-
1304	Unimproved	-	Langdon	Woodbury	-	-	-
1305	Unimproved	-	Langdon	Woodbury	-	-	-
1306	Unimproved	-	Langdon	Woodbury	-	-	-
1307	Unimproved	-	Langdon	Woodbury	-	-	-
1308	Unimproved	-	Langdon	Woodbury	-	-	-
1309	Unimproved	-	Langdon	Woodbury	-	-	-
1310	Unimproved	-	Langdon	Woodbury	-	-	-
1311	Unimproved	-	Langdon	Woodbury	-	-	-
1312	Unimproved	-	Langdon	Woodbury	-	-	-
1313	Unimproved	-	Langdon	Woodbury	-	-	-
1314	Unimproved	-	Langdon	Woodbury	-	-	-
1315	Unimproved	-	Langdon	Woodbury	-	-	-
1316	Unimproved	-	Langdon	Woodbury	-	-	-
1317	Unimproved	-	Langdon	Woodbury	-	-	-
1318	Unimproved	-	Langdon	Woodbury	-	-	-
1319	Unimproved	-	Langdon	Woodbury	-	-	-
1320	Unimproved	-	Langdon	Woodbury	-	-	-

NEW HAMPSHIRE DISTRICT 13

Pg/No	Ext Per	Acr	Per	Property Location	Residence of Owner	Value $	Eq. Val $	Total $
1126	-	100	-	Tuftonboro	Tuftonboro	150.00	186.00	1413.60
1201	-	100	-	Tuftonboro	Tuftonboro	150.00	186.00	-
1202	-	100	-	Tuftonboro	Tuftonboro	150.00	186.00	-
1203	-	100	-	Tuftonboro	Tuftonboro	150.00	186.00	-
1204	-	100	-	Tuftonboro	Tuftonboro	150.00	186.00	-
1205	-	100	-	Tuftonboro	Tuftonboro	150.00	186.00	-
1206	-	100	-	Tuftonboro	Tuftonboro	150.00	186.00	-
1207	-	100	-	Tuftonboro	Tuftonboro	179.00	221.96	-
1208	-	50	-	Tuftonboro	Tuftonboro	50.00	62.00	-
1209	-	100	-	Tuftonboro	Tuftonboro	75.00	93.00	-
1210	-	48	-	Tuftonboro	Tuftonboro	75.00	93.00	-
1211	-	55	-	Tuftonboro	Tuftonboro	50.00	62.00	1647.96
1212	-	70	-	Tuftonboro	Brookfield	210.00	260.40	260.40
1213	-	14	-	Tuftonboro	Tuftonboro	61.00	75.64	75.64
1214	-	100	-	Tuftonboro	Tuftonboro	200.00	248.00	248.00
1215	-	50	-	Tuftonboro	Tuftonboro	250.00	310.00	310.00
1216	-	100	-	Tuftonboro	Tuftonboro	370.00	458.80	458.80
1217	-	1000	-	Tuftonboro	Portsmouth	2000.00	2480.00	2480.00
1218	-	500	-	Tuftonboro	Portsmouth	1500.00	1860.00	-
1219	-	100	-	Tuftonboro	Tuftonboro	150.00	186.00	-
1220	-	88	-	Tuftonboro	Tuftonboro	120.00	148.80	-
1221	-	100	-	Tuftonboro	Tuftonboro	120.00	148.80	-
1222	-	100	-	Tuftonboro	Tuftonboro	100.00	124.00	-
1223	-	100	-	Tuftonboro	Tuftonboro	100.00	124.00	-
1224	-	100	-	Tuftonboro	Tuftonboro	150.00	186.00	-
1225	-	110	-	Tuftonboro	Tuftonboro	300.00	372.00	-
1226	-	100	-	Tuftonboro	Tuftonboro	150.00	186.00	3335.60
1301	-	100	-	Tuftonboro	Portsmouth	250.00	310.00	-
1302	-	26	-	Tuftonboro	Tuftonboro	50.00	62.00	-
1303	-	142	-	Tuftonboro	Tuftonboro	300.00	372.00	-
1304	-	45	-	Tuftonboro	Tuftonboro	45.00	55.80	-
1305	-	100	-	Tuftonboro	Tuftonboro	250.00	310.00	-
1306	-	100	-	Tuftonboro	Tuftonboro	150.00	186.00	-
1307	-	100	-	Tuftonboro	Tuftonboro	150.00	186.00	-
1308	-	100	-	Tuftonboro	Tuftonboro	125.00	155.00	-
1309	-	100	-	Tuftonboro	Tuftonboro	100.00	124.00	-
1310	-	50	-	Tuftonboro	Tuftonboro	50.00	62.00	-
1311	-	100	-	Tuftonboro	Tuftonboro	200.00	248.00	-
1312	-	100	-	Tuftonboro	Tuftonboro	200.00	248.00	-
1313	-	100	-	Tuftonboro	Tuftonboro	100.00	124.00	-
1314	-	59	-	Tuftonboro	Tuftonboro	50.00	62.00	-
1315	-	100	-	Tuftonboro	Tuftonboro	126.00	156.24	-
1316	-	96	-	Tuftonboro	Tuftonboro	50.00	62.00	-
1317	-	100	-	Tuftonboro	Tuftonboro	250.00	310.00	-
1318	-	100	-	Tuftonboro	Tuftonboro	150.00	186.00	-
1319	-	100	-	Tuftonboro	Tuftonboro	150.00	186.00	-
1320	-	44	-	Tuftonboro	Tuftonboro	50.00	62.00	-

1798 DIRECT TAX

Pg/No	Occupant Surname	Occupant First Name	Owner Surname	Owner First Name	Dwg #	Val $	Expt Acr
1321	Unimproved	-	Langdon	Woodbury	-	-	-
1322	Unimproved	-	Langdon	Woodbury	-	-	-
1323	Unimproved	-	Langdon	Woodbury	-	-	-
1324	Unimproved	-	Langdon	Woodbury	-	-	-
1325	Unimproved	-	Langdon	Woodbury	-	-	-
1326	Unimproved	-	Langdon	Woodbury	-	-	-
1401	Unimproved	-	Langdon	Woodbury	-	-	-
1402	Unimproved	-	Langdon	Woodbury	-	-	-
1403	Unimproved	-	Langdon	Woodbury	-	-	-
1404	Unimproved	-	Langdon	Woodbury	-	-	-
1405	Unimproved	-	Langdon	Woodbury	-	-	-
1406	Unimproved	-	Langdon	Woodbury	-	-	-
1407	Unimproved	-	Langdon	Woodbury	-	-	-
1408	Unimproved	-	Langdon	Woodbury	-	-	-
1409	Unimproved	-	Langdon	Woodbury	-	-	-
1410	Unimproved	-	Langdon	Woodbury	-	-	-
1411	Unimproved	-	Langdon	Woodbury	-	-	-
1412	Unimproved	-	Langdon	Woodbury	-	-	-
1413	Unimproved	-	Langdon	Woodbury	-	-	-
1414	Unimproved	-	Langdon	Woodbury	-	-	-
1415	Unimproved	-	Langdon	Woodbury	-	-	-
1416	Unimproved	-	Langdon	Woodbury	-	-	-
1417	Unimproved	-	Langdon	Woodbury	-	-	-
1418	Unimproved	-	Langdon	Woodbury	-	-	-
1419	Unimproved	-	Langdon	Woodbury	-	-	-
1420	Unimproved	-	Langdon	Woodbury	-	-	-
1421	Unimproved	-	Langdon	Woodbury	-	-	-
1422	Unimproved	-	Langdon	Woodbury	-	-	-
1423	Unimproved	-	Langdon	Woodbury	-	-	-
1424	Unimproved	-	Moffatt	Mrs. C.	-	-	-
1425	Maloon	Isaiah L.	Meloon	Isaiah L.	-	-	-
1426	Moody	Josiah	Moody	Josiah	-	-	-
1501	McIntire	Ebenezer	McIntire	Ebenezer	1	20	-
1502	McIntire	Joshua	McIntire	Joshua	-	-	-
1503	McIntire	William	McIntire	William	-	-	-
1504	Unimproved	-	Marden	James	-	-	-
1505	Mallard	William	Meader	Ebenezer	1	60	-
1506	Unimproved	-	Mallard	William	-	-	-
1507	Brown	Obadiah	Nutter	Samuel	1	15	-
1508	Nutter	Grafton	Nutter	Grafton	-	-	-
1509	Unimproved	-	Nute	Thomas	-	-	-
1510	Unimproved	-	Perkins	John	-	-	-
1511	Peirce	Benjamin	Peirce	Benjamin	-	-	-
1512	Piper	Samuel	Piper	Samuel	-	-	-
1513	-	-	Peavey	Joseph	1	30	-
1514	-	-	Peavey	Joseph	-	-	-
1515	-	-	Peavey	Joseph	-	-	-

NEW HAMPSHIRE DISTRICT 13

Pg/No	Ext Per	Acr	Per	Property Location	Residence of Owner	Value $	Eq. Val $	Total $
1321	-	100	-	Tuftonboro	Tuftonboro	150.00	186.00	-
1322	-	100	-	Tuftonboro	Tuftonboro	150.00	186.00	-
1323	-	100	-	Tuftonboro	Tuftonboro	150.00	186.00	-
1324	-	100	-	Tuftonboro	Tuftonboro	250.00	310.00	-
1325	-	100	-	Tuftonboro	Tuftonboro	250.00	310.00	-
1326	-	100	-	Tuftonboro	Tuftonboro	100.00	124.00	4769.04
1401	-	100	-	Tuftonboro	Portsmouth	150.00	186.00	-
1402	-	100	-	Tuftonboro	Tuftonboro	150.00	186.00	-
1403	-	39	-	Tuftonboro	Tuftonboro	39.00	48.36	-
1404	-	100	-	Tuftonboro	Tuftonboro	125.00	155.00	-
1405	-	100	-	Tuftonboro	Tuftonboro	250.00	310.00	-
1406	-	100	-	Tuftonboro	Tuftonboro	100.00	124.00	-
1407	-	100	-	Tuftonboro	Tuftonboro	150.00	186.00	-
1408	-	100	-	Tuftonboro	Tuftonboro	150.00	186.00	-
1409	-	100	-	Tuftonboro	Tuftonboro	250.00	310.00	-
1410	-	100	-	Tuftonboro	Tuftonboro	100.00	124.00	-
1411	-	100	-	Tuftonboro	Tuftonboro	100.00	124.00	-
1412	-	100	-	Tuftonboro	Tuftonboro	100.00	124.00	-
1413	-	100	-	Tuftonboro	Tuftonboro	100.00	124.00	-
1414	-	100	-	Tuftonboro	Tuftonboro	100.00	124.00	-
1415	-	100	-	Tuftonboro	Tuftonboro	100.00	124.00	-
1416	-	100	-	Tuftonboro	Tuftonboro	100.00	124.00	-
1417	-	100	-	Tuftonboro	Tuftonboro	100.00	124.00	-
1418	-	100	-	Tuftonboro	Tuftonboro	100.00	124.00	-
1419	-	82	-	Tuftonboro	Tuftonboro	100.00	124.00	-
1420	-	55	-	Tuftonboro	Tuftonboro	50.00	62.00	-
1421	-	94	-	Tuftonboro	Tuftonboro	50.00	62.00	-
1422	-	87	-	Tuftonboro	Tuftonboro	100.00	124.00	-
1423	-	100	-	Tuftonboro	Tuftonboro	150.00	186.00	3365.36
1424	-	500	-	Tuftonboro	Portsmouth	250.00	310.00	310.00
1425	-	45	-	Tuftonboro	Tuftonboro	160.00	198.40	198.40
1426	-	25	-	Tuftonboro	Tuftonboro	100.00	124.00	124.00
1501	-	80	-	Tuftonboro	Tuftonboro	360.00	446.40	446.40
1502	-	30	-	Tuftonboro	Tuftonboro	100.00	124.00	124.00
1503	-	50	-	Tuftonboro	Tuftonboro	130.00	161.20	161.20
1504	-	100	-	Tuftonboro	Wolfeboro	300.00	372.00	372.00
1505	-	55	-	Tuftonboro	Wolfeboro	225.00	279.00	279.00
1506	-	20	-	Tuftonboro	Tuftonboro	50.00	62.00	62.00
1507	-	100	-	Tuftonboro	Portsmouth	565.00	700.60	700.60
1508	-	60	-	Tuftonboro	Tuftonboro	285.00	353.40	353.40
1509	-	50	-	Tuftonboro	Wolfeboro	75.00	93.00	93.00
1510	-	20	-	Tuftonboro	Wakefield	50.00	62.00	62.00
1511	-	46	-	Tuftonboro	Tuftonboro	161.00	199.64	199.64
1512	-	50	-	Tuftonboro	Tuftonboro	190.00	235.60	235.60
1513	-	50	-	Tuftonboro	Tuftonboro	150.00	186.00	-
1514	-	100	-	Tuftonboro	Tuftonboro	300.00	372.00	-
1515	-	25	-	Tuftonboro	Tuftonboro	75.00	93.00	651.00

1798 DIRECT TAX

Pg/No	Occupant Surname	Occupant First Name	Owner Surname	Owner First Name	Dwg #	Val $	Expt Acr
1516	Piper	Timothy	Piper	Timothy	-	-	-
1517	Pinkham	Joseph & Benj.	Pinkham	Joseph & Benj.	1	25	-
1518	Pinkham	Edmund	Pinkham	Edmund	-	-	-
1519	Unimproved	-	Page	Josiah	-	-	-
1520	Unimproved	-	Peirce	John	-	-	-
1521	Unimproved	-	Peirce	John	-	-	-
1522	Unimproved	-	Rendall	William	-	-	-
1523	Unimproved	-	Robinson	Abednego	-	-	-
1524	Unimproved	-	Sheafe	James	-	-	-
1525	Unimproved	-	Sheafe	James	-	-	-
1526	Unimproved	-	Sheafe	James	-	-	-
1601	Unimproved	-	Sheafe	James	-	-	-
1602	Unimproved	-	Sheafe	James	-	-	-
1603	Unimproved	-	Sheafe	James	-	-	-
1604	Unimproved	-	Sheafe	James	-	-	-
1605	Unimproved	-	Sheafe	James	-	-	-
1606	Unimproved	-	Sheafe	James	-	-	-
1607		-	Stevens	Enoch	-	-	-
1608	Unimproved	-	Taylor	Heirs of Joseph	-	-	-
1609	Unimproved	-	Sweat	Solomon Ricker	-	-	-
1610	Thomas	Enoch	Thomas	Enoch	1	10	-
1611	Thing	Winthrop	Thing	Winthrop	1	25	-
1612	Unimproved	-	Whipple	Joseph	-	-	-
1613	Wille	Samuel	Wille	Samuel	-	-	-
1614	Wiggin	James	Wiggin	James	-	-	-
1615	Wiggin	Andrew	Wiggin	Andrew	1	30	-
1616	Wiggin	Benjamin	Wiggin	Benjamin	-	-	-
1617	Wiggin	Henry & Henry J	Wiggin	Henry & Henry J	-	-	-
1618	Warren	William	Warren	William	1	20	-
1619	Whitehouse	James	Whitehouse	James	-	-	-
1620	Young	Benjamin	Young	Benjamin	1	30	-
1621	Young	Timothy	Young	Timothy	1	10	-
1622	Allen	Abner	Allen	Abner	-	-	-
1623	Allen	Josiah	Allen	Josiah	-	-	-
1624	Allen	Samuel	Allen	Samuel	-	-	-
1625	Babb	Charles	Babb	Charles	1	20	-
1626	Ballard	Frederick	Ballard	Frederick	-	-	-
1627	Ballard	Frederick	Ballard	Frederick	-	-	-
1701	Blasdell	William W.	Blasdell	William W.	-	-	-
1702	Unimproved	-	Boardman	Benjamin, Jr.	-	-	-
1703	Unimproved	-	Boardman	Benjamin, Jr.	-	-	-
1704	Brown	Benjamin	Brown	Benjamin	1	5	-
1705	Bryant	James	Bryant	James	1	10	-
1706	Burleigh	Jonathan	Burleigh	Jonathan	-	-	-
1707	Chapman	Samuel	Chapman	Samuel	-	-	-
1708	Clark	Jacob	Clark	Jacob	-	-	-
1709	Clark	Jacob	Clark	Est. of Mayhu	1	10	-

NEW HAMPSHIRE DISTRICT 13

Pg/No	Ext Per	Acr	Per	Property Location	Residence of Owner	Value $	Eq. Val $	Total $
1516	-	60	-	Tuftonboro	Tuftonboro	200.00	248.00	248.00
1517	-	100	-	Tuftonboro	Tuftonboro	400.00	496.00	496.00
1518	-	50	-	Tuftonboro	Tuftonboro	150.00	186.00	186.00
1519	-	50	-	Tuftonboro	Wakefield	150.00	186.00	186.00
1520	-	1200	-	Tuftonboro	Portsmouth	2400.00	2976.00	-
1521	-	40	-	Tuftonboro	Tuftonboro	80.00	99.20	3075.20
1522	-	50	-	Tuftonboro	Wakefield	150.00	186.00	186.00
1523	-	100	-	Tuftonboro	Gilmanton	300.00	372.00	372.00
1524	-	100	-	Tuftonboro	Portsmouth	100.00	124.00	-
1525	-	100	-	Tuftonboro	Tuftonboro	200.00	248.00	-
1526	-	100	-	Tuftonboro	Tuftonboro	150.00	186.00	558.00
1601	-	100	-	Tuftonboro	Portsmouth	50.00	62.00	-
1602	-	100	-	Tuftonboro	Tuftonboro	50.00	62.00	-
1603	-	100	-	Tuftonboro	Tuftonboro	150.00	186.00	-
1604	-	100	-	Tuftonboro	Tuftonboro	100.00	124.00	-
1605	-	88	-	Tuftonboro	Tuftonboro	44.00	54.56	-
1606	-	500	-	Tuftonboro	Tuftonboro	250.00	310.00	798.56
1607	-	50	-	Tuftonboro	Lee	150.00	186.00	186.00
1608	-	1000	-	Tuftonboro	Boston, MA	500.00	620.00	620.00
1609	-	100	-	Tuftonboro	Tuftonboro	200.00	248.00	248.00
1610	-	100	-	Tuftonboro	Tuftonboro	440.00	545.60	545.60
1611	-	50	-	Tuftonboro	Tuftonboro	250.00	310.00	310.00
1612	-	100	-	Tuftonboro	Portsmouth	200.00	248.00	248.00
1613	-	50	-	Tuftonboro	Tuftonboro	125.00	155.00	155.00
1614	-	100	-	Tuftonboro	Tuftonboro	300.00	372.00	372.00
1615	-	100	-	Tuftonboro	Tuftonboro	400.00	496.00	496.00
1616	-	50	-	Tuftonboro	Tuftonboro	175.00	217.00	217.00
1617	-	399	-	Tuftonboro	Tuftonboro	1700.00	2108.00	2108.00
1618	-	61	-	Tuftonboro	Tuftonboro	160.00	198.40	198.40
1619	-	100	-	Tuftonboro	Tuftonboro	150.00	186.00	186.00
1620	-	100	-	Tuftonboro	Tuftonboro	400.00	496.00	496.00
1621	-	10	-	Tuftonboro	Tuftonboro	150.00	186.00	186.00
1622	-	75	-	Wakefield	Wakefield	340.00	421.60	421.60
1623	-	98	-	Wakefield	Wakefield	336.00	416.64	416.64
1624	-	90	-	Wakefield	Wakefield	375.00	465.00	465.00
1625	-	55	-	Wakefield	Wakefield	150.00	186.00	186.00
1626	-	29	-	Wakefield	Wakefield	189.00	234.36	-
1627	-	150	-	Wakefield	Wakefield	400.00	496.00	730.36
1701	-	100	-	Wakefield	Wakefield	656.00	813.44	813.44
1702	-	100	-	Wakefield	Exeter	84.00	104.16	-
1703	-	100	-	Wakefield	Wakefield	126.00	156.24	260.40
1704	-	45	-	Wakefield	Wakefield	70.00	86.80	86.80
1705	-	55	-	Wakefield	Wakefield	185.00	229.40	229.40
1706	-	144	-	Wakefield	Wakefield	600.00	744.00	744.00
1707	-	125	-	Wakefield	Wakefield	640.00	793.60	793.60
1708	-	200	-	Wakefield	Wakefield	900.00	1116.00	1116.00
1709	-	100	-	Wakefield	Wakefield	475.00	589.00	-

1798 DIRECT TAX

Pg/No	Occupant Surname	Occupant First Name	Owner Surname	Owner First Name	Dwg #	Val $	Expt Acr
1710	Clark	Jacob	Clark	Est. of Mayhu	-	-	-
1711	Cloutman	Thomas	Cloutman	Thomas	-	-	-
1712	Unimproved	-	Cogswell	Amos	-	-	-
1713	Colby	Moses	Colby	Moses	1	60	-
1714	Cook	Ebenezer	Cook	Ebenezer	-	-	-
1715	Cook	Jonathan	Cook	Jonathan	1	15	-
1716	Cook	Nathaniel	Cook	Nathaniel	-	-	-
1717	Cook	Nathaniel	Cook	Nathaniel	-	-	-
1718	Cook	Peter	Cook	Peter	-	-	-
1719	Copp	David	Copp	David	-	-	-
1720	Copp	David	Copp	David	-	-	-
1721	Unimproved	-	Copp	David	-	-	-
1722	Unimproved	-	Copp	David	-	-	-
1723	Unimproved	-	Copp	David	-	-	-
1724	Unimproved	-	Copp	David	-	-	-
1725	Unimproved	-	Copp	David	-	-	-
1726	Unimproved	-	Copp	David	-	-	-
1801	Unimproved	-	Copp	David	-	-	-
1802	Unimproved	-	Copp	David	-	-	-
1803	Unimproved	-	Copp	David	-	-	-
1804	Unimproved	-	Copp	David	-	-	-
1805	Copp	Moses	Copp	Moses	-	-	-
1806	Copp	Moses	Cutts	Samuel	-	-	-
1807	Copp	Moses	Chamberlain	William	-	-	-
1808	Dearborn	Benjamin	Dearborn	Benjamin	-	-	-
1809	Dearborn	Jeremiah	Dearborn	Jeremiah	-	-	-
1810	Unimproved	-	Dearborn	Joseph	-	-	-
1811	Dearborn	Nathan	Dearborn	Nathan	1	10	-
1812	Dearborn	Nathan	Dearborn	Samuel	-	-	-
1813	Dow	Richard	Dow	Richard	-	-	-
1814	Edgerly	Joshua	Edgerly	Joshua	1	25	-
1815	Fellows	Isaac	Fellows	Isaac	1	80	-
1816	Fellows	Isaac	Fellows	Moses	-	-	-
1817	Unimproved	-	Folson	Eliz	-	-	-
1818	Gage	Moses	Gage	Moses	1	70	-
1819	Garland	John	Garland	John	-	-	-
1820	Garvin	Ebenezer	Garvin	Ebenezer	-	-	-
1821	Unimproved	-	Gage	Joseph	-	-	-
1822	Gilman	Andrew	Gilman	Andrew	-	-	-
1823	Unimproved	-	Gilman	Andrew	-	-	-
1824	Unimproved	-	Gilman	Andrew	-	-	-
1825	Gilman	Dudley	Gilman	Dudley	-	-	-
1826	Gilman	John	Gilman	John	-	-	-
1901	Hall	Avery	Hall	Avery	-	-	-
1902	Hall	Avery	Hall	Avery	-	-	-
1903	Hall	Benjamin	Hall	Benjamin	-	-	-
1904	Hall	Daniel	Hall	Daniel	-	-	-

NEW HAMPSHIRE DISTRICT 13

Pg/No	Ext Per	Acr	Per	Property Location	Residence of Owner	Value $	Eq. Val $	Total $
1710	-	200	-	Wakefield	Wakefield	100.00	124.00	713.00
1711	-	200	-	Wakefield	Wakefield	500.00	620.00	620.00
1712	-	110	-	Wakefield	Dover	84.00	104.16	104.16
1713	-	40	-	Wakefield	Wakefield	245.00	303.80	303.80
1714	-	45	-	Wakefield	Wakefield	225.00	279.00	279.00
1715	-	30	-	Wakefield	Wakefield	130.00	161.20	161.20
1716	-	90	-	Wakefield	Wakefield	365.00	452.60	-
1717	-	165	-	Wakefield	Wakefield	200.00	248.00	700.60
1718	-	174	-	Wakefield	Wakefield	300.00	372.00	372.00
1719	-	320	-	Wakefield	Wakefield	1700.00	2108.00	-
1720	-	258	-	Wakefield	Wakefield	1758.00	2179.92	-
1721	-	110	-	Wakefield	Wakefield	110.00	136.40	-
1722	-	40	-	Wakefield	Wakefield	40.00	49.60	-
1723	-	30	-	Wakefield	Wakefield	30.00	37.20	-
1724	-	50	-	Wakefield	Wakefield	50.00	62.00	-
1725	-	50	-	Wakefield	Wakefield	50.00	62.00	-
1726	-	20	-	Wakefield	Wakefield	20.00	24.80	4659.92
1801	-	25	-	Wakefield	Wakefield	25.00	31.00	-
1802	-	110	-	Wakefield	Wakefield	110.00	136.40	-
1803	-	55	-	Wakefield	Wakefield	55.00	68.20	-
1804	-	100	-	Wakefield	Wakefield	100.00	124.00	359.60
1805	-	150	-	Wakefield	Wakefield	300.00	372.00	372.00
1806	-	100	-	Wakefield	Portsmouth	100.00	124.00	124.00
1807	-	50	-	Wakefield	Brookfield	100.00	124.00	124.00
1808	-	56	-	Wakefield	Wakefield	392.00	486.08	486.08
1809	-	100	-	Wakefield	Wakefield	490.00	607.60	607.60
1810	-	90	-	Wakefield	North Hampton	90.00	111.60	111.60
1811	-	70	-	Wakefield	Wakefield	405.00	502.20	502.20
1812	-	100	-	Wakefield	North Hampton	300.00	372.00	372.00
1813	-	110	-	Wakefield	Wakefield	710.00	880.40	880.40
1814	-	100	-	Wakefield	Wakefield	400.00	496.00	496.00
1815	-	127	-	Wakefield	Wakefield	922.00	1143.28	1143.28
1816	-	9	-	Wakefield	Wakefield	45.00	55.80	55.80
1817	-	100	-	Wakefield	Exeter	42.00	52.08	52.08
1818	-	80	-	Wakefield	Wakefield	460.00	570.40	570.40
1819	-	100	-	Wakefield	Wakefield	535.00	663.40	663.40
1820	-	137	-	Wakefield	Wakefield	574.00	711.76	711.76
1821	-	100	-	Wakefield	Dover	25.00	31.00	31.00
1822	-	80	-	Wakefield	Wakefield	610.00	756.40	-
1823	-	110	-	Wakefield	Wakefield	50.00	62.00	-
1824	-	25	-	Wakefield	Wakefield	75.00	93.00	911.40
1825	-	100	-	Wakefield	Wakefield	640.00	793.60	793.60
1826	-	190	-	Wakefield	Wakefield	1010.00	1252.40	1252.40
1901	-	375	-	Wakefield	Wakefield	1700.00	2108.00	-
1902	-	250	-	Wakefield	Wakefield	125.00	155.00	2263.00
1903	-	60	-	Wakefield	Wakefield	90.00	111.60	111.60
1904	-	208	-	Wakefield	Wakefield	880.00	1091.20	1091.20

1798 DIRECT TAX

Pg/No	Occupant Surname	Occupant First Name	Owner Surname	Owner First Name	Dwg #	Val $	Expt Acr
1905	Hall	Daniel	Hall	Samuel	-	-	-
1906	Hall	Daniel	Hall	Samuel	-	-	-
1907	Hall	Daniel	Hall	Samuel	-	-	-
1908	Hall	Daniel	Hall	Samuel	-	-	-
1909	Hall	Daniel	Hall	Samuel	-	-	-
1910	Haines	Joseph	Haines	Joseph	-	-	-
1911	Hanson	Tobias	Hanson	Tobias	-	-	-
1912	Hardy	Robert	Hardy	Robert	-	-	-
1913	Hawkins	Stephen	Hawkins	Stephen	1	30	-
1914	Hill	Ebenezer	Hill	Ebenezer	1	40	-
1915	Hill	Reuben	Hill	Reuben	1	90	-
1916	Hodgdon	Joseph	Hodgdon	Joseph	-	-	-
1917	Horn	Daniel	Horn	Daniel	1	60	-
1918	Horn	Daniel	Horn	Daniel	-	-	-
1919	Horn	David	Horn	David	1	20	-
1920	Horn	John	Horn	John	-	-	-
1921	Horn	John	Horn	John	-	-	-
1922	Huggin	John	Huggin	John	1	10	-
1923	Unimproved	-	Hurd	Samuel	-	-	-
1924	Hutchins	James	Hutchins	James	-	-	-
1925	Hutchins	Solomon	Hutchins	Solomon	-	-	-
1926	Unimproved	-	Inhabitants	-	-	-	100
1927	Unimproved	-	Inhabitants	-	-	-	110
1928	Unimproved	-	Inhabitants	-	-	-	110
2001	Johnson	John	Johnson	John	1	60	-
2002	-	-	Kennison	Waldron	-	-	-
2003	Kimball	John	Kimball	John	-	-	-
2004	Kimball	John	Kimball	John	-	-	-
2005	Kimball	Noah	Kimball	Noah	-	-	-
2006	Kimball	Noah	Kimball	Noah	-	-	-
2007	Lang	Reuben	Lang	Reuben	-	-	-
2008	Lang	Reuben	Lang	Reuben	-	-	-
2009	Leavitt	Joseph	Leavitt	Joseph	-	-	-
2010	Leavitt	Joseph	Leavitt	Joseph	-	-	-
2011	Leavitt	Joseph	Leavitt	Joseph	-	-	-
2012	Leavitt	Joseph	Leavitt	Joseph	-	-	-
2013	Leavitt	Joseph	Leavitt	Joseph	-	-	-
2014	Leavitt	Joseph	Leavitt	Joseph	-	-	-
2015	Leavitt	Joseph	Leavitt	Joseph	-	-	-
2016	Leavitt	Joseph	Leavitt	Joseph	-	-	-
2017	Lindsey	Thomas	Lindsey	Thomas	-	-	-
2018	Locke	Jacob	Locke	Jacob	1	90	-
2019	Unimproved	-	Locke	Jacob	-	-	-
2020	Mailham	Joseph	Mailham	Joseph	-	-	-
2021	-	-	Marsh	John	-	-	-
2022	Merrow	Moses	Merrow	Moses	-	-	-
2023	Manning	John	Manning	John	-	-	-

NEW HAMPSHIRE DISTRICT 13

Pg/No	Ext Per	Acr	Per	Property Location	Residence of Owner	Value $	Eq. Val $	Total $
1905	-	90	-	Wakefield	Wakefield	180.00	223.20	-
1906	-	100	-	Wakefield	Wakefield	200.00	248.00	-
1907	-	100	-	Wakefield	Wakefield	200.00	248.00	-
1908	-	50	-	Wakefield	Wakefield	100.00	124.00	-
1909	-	50	-	Wakefield	Wakefield	100.00	124.00	967.20
1910	-	80	-	Wakefield	Wakefield	385.00	477.40	447.40
1911	-	100	-	Wakefield	Wakefield	490.00	607.60	607.60
1912	-	75	-	Wakefield	Wakefield	300.00	372.00	372.00
1913	-	110	-	Wakefield	Wakefield	440.00	545.60	545.60
1914	-	125	-	Wakefield	Wakefield	370.00	458.80	458.80
1915	-	50	-	Wakefield	Wakefield	460.00	570.40	570.40
1916	-	115	-	Wakefield	Wakefield	595.00	737.80	737.80
1917	-	30	-	Wakefield	Wakefield	210.00	260.40	-
1918	-	40	-	Wakefield	Wakefield	80.00	99.20	359.60
1919	-	100	-	Wakefield	Wakefield	400.00	496.00	496.00
1920	-	100	-	Wakefield	Wakefield	500.00	620.00	-
1921	-	55	-	Wakefield	Wakefield	50.00	62.00	682.00
1922	-	50	-	Wakefield	Wakefield	205.00	254.20	254.20
1923	-	110	-	Wakefield	Dover	110.00	136.40	136.40
1924	-	176	-	Wakefield	Wakefield	711.00	881.64	881.64
1925	-	70	-	Wakefield	Wakefield	305.00	378.20	378.20
1926	-	-	-	Wakefield	Wakefield	-	-	-
1927	-	-	-	Wakefield	Wakefield	-	-	-
1928	-	-	-	Wakefield	Wakefield	-	-	-
2001	-	114	-	Wakefield	Wakefield	660.00	818.40	818.40
2002	-	40	-	Wakefield	Brookfield	80.00	99.20	99.20
2003	-	170	-	Wakefield	Wakefield	1080.00	1339.20	-
2004	-	25	-	Wakefield	Wakefield	100.00	124.00	1463.20
2005	-	124	-	Wakefield	Wakefield	978.00	1212.72	-
2006	-	10	-	Wakefield	Wakefield	40.00	49.60	1262.32
2007	-	50	-	Wakefield	Wakefield	300.00	372.00	-
2008	-	10	-	Wakefield	Wakefield	60.00	74.40	446.40
2009	-	100	-	Wakefield	Wakefield	830.00	1029.20	-
2010	-	200	-	Wakefield	Wakefield	400.00	496.00	-
2011	-	125	-	Wakefield	Wakefield	250.00	310.00	-
2012	-	100	-	Wakefield	Wakefield	200.00	248.00	-
2013	-	110	-	Wakefield	Wakefield	220.00	272.80	-
2014	-	110	-	Wakefield	Wakefield	220.00	272.80	-
2015	-	110	-	Wakefield	Wakefield	220.00	272.80	-
2016	-	30	-	Wakefield	Wakefield	60.00	74.40	2976.00
2017	-	23	-	Wakefield	Wakefield	112.00	138.88	133.88
2018	-	6	-	Wakefield	Wakefield	180.00	223.20	-
2019	-	47	-	Wakefield	Wakefield	94.00	116.56	339.76
2020	-	80	-	Wakefield	Wakefield	500.00	620.00	620.00
2021	-	81	-	Wakefield	Barrington	81.00	100.44	100.44
2022	-	40	-	Wakefield	Wakefield	160.00	198.40	198.40
2023	-	39	-	Wakefield	Wakefield	200.00	248.00	248.00

1798 DIRECT TAX

Pg/No	Occupant Surname	Occupant First Name	Owner Surname	Owner First Name	Dwg #	Val $	Expt Acr
2024	Mordough	Robert	Mordough	Robert	-	-	-
2025	Moulton	Robert	Moulton	Robert	-	-	-
2026	Neal	Levi	Neal	Levi	-	-	-
2101	Nudd	Simon	Nudd	Simon	1	20	-
2102	Nudd	Thomas	Nudd	Thomas	-	-	-
2103	Piper	Asa	Piper	Asa	-	-	125
2104	Piper	Asa	Piper	Asa	-	-	110
2105	Palmer	Jonathan	Palmer	Jonathan	-	-	-
2106	Palmer	Jonathan	Palmer	Jonathan	-	-	-
2107	Unimproved	-	Palmer	Jonathan	-	-	-
2108	Unimproved	-	Palmer	Jonathan	-	-	-
2109	Unimproved	-	Palmer	Jonathan	-	-	-
2110	Unimproved	-	Palmer	William	-	-	-
2111	Page	Josiah	Page	Josiah	1	30	-
2112	Page	Josiah	Page	Josiah	-	-	-
2113	Perkins	Daniel	Perkins	Daniel	-	-	-
2114	Perkins	Nathaniel	Perkins	Nathaniel	1	20	-
2115	Perkins	Thomas	Perkins	Thomas	1	30	-
2116	Philbrick	Eliphalet	Philbrick	Eliphalet	-	-	-
2117	Unimproved	-	Philbrick	Eliphalet	-	-	-
2118	Pike	Joseph	Pike	Joseph	1	40	-
2119	-	-	Perkins	B.	1	90	-
2120	-	-	Perkins	Benjamin, Jr.	1	80	-
2121	Quimby	Eliphalet	Quimby	Eliphalet	-	-	-
2122	Quimby	Jonathan	Quimby	Jonathan	1	20	-
2123	Unimproved	-	Richardson	Joseph	-	-	-
2124	Unimproved	-	Richardson	Joseph	-	-	-
2125	Roberts	Nathaniel	Roberts	Nathaniel	-	-	-
2126	Rundlet	Joshua	Rundlet	Joshua	1	90	-
2127	Safford	Benjamin	Safford	Benjamin	-	-	-
2128	Safford	Benjamin	Safford	Benjamin	-	-	-
2201	Sanborn	Daniel	Sanborn	Daniel	1	30	-
2202	Sanborn	Elisha	Sanborn	Elisha	-	-	-
2203	Sanborn	John	Sanborn	John	1	80	-
2204	Sanborn	Jacob	Sanborn	Jacob	1	50	-
2205	Sanborn	Reuben	Sanborn	Reuben	1	30	-
2206	-	-	Seammon	James	-	-	-
2207	Scates	Ithiel	Scates	Ithiel	1	80	-
2208	Scates	Ithiel	Scates	Ithiel	-	-	-
2209	Shannon	Thomas	Shannon	Thomas	-	-	-
2210	Shannon	Thomas	Shannon	Thomas	-	-	-
2211	Sherburne	Samuel	Sherburne	Samuel	1	10	-
2212	Skinner	Christopher	Skinner	Christopher	1	20	-
2213	Thurston	Thomas	Thurston	Thomas	1	30	-
2214	Paul	Samuel	Unknown	-	-	-	-
2215	Watson	John	Watson	John	1	20	-
2216	Watson	Jonathan	Watson	Jonathan	1	30	-

NEW HAMPSHIRE DISTRICT 13

Pg/No	Ext Per	Acr	Per	Property Location	Residence of Owner	Value $	Eq. Val $	Total $
2024	-	81	-	Wakefield	Wakefield	586.00	726.64	726.64
2025	-	10	-	Wakefield	Middleton	40.00	49.60	49.60
2026	-	100	-	Wakefield	Wakefield	660.00	818.40	818.40
2101	-	70	-	Wakefield	Wakefield	250.00	310.00	310.00
2102	-	80	-	Wakefield	Wakefield	300.00	372.00	372.00
2103	-	-	-	Wakefield	Wakefield	-	-	-
2104	-	-	-	Wakefield	Wakefield	-	-	-
2105	-	100	-	Wakefield	Wakefield	680.00	843.20	-
2106	-	30	-	Wakefield	Wakefield	30.00	37.20	-
2107	-	100	-	Wakefield	Wakefield	100.00	124.00	-
2108	-	100	-	Wakefield	Wakefield	100.00	124.00	-
2109	-	100	-	Wakefield	Wakefield	100.00	124.00	1252.40
2110	-	100	-	Wakefield	Rochester	100.00	124.00	124.00
2111	-	60	-	Wakefield	Wakefield	500.00	620.00	-
2112	-	75	-	Wakefield	Wakefield	336.00	416.64	1036.64
2113	-	0	120	Wakefield	Wakefield	30.00	37.20	37.20
2114	-	55	-	Wakefield	Wakefield	220.00	272.80	272.80
2115	-	60	-	Wakefield	Wakefield	200.00	248.00	248.00
2116	-	95	-	Wakefield	Wakefield	715.00	886.60	-
2117	-	42	-	Wakefield	Wakefield	168.00	208.32	1094.92
2118	-	60	-	Wakefield	Wakefield	280.00	347.20	347.20
2119	-	50	-	Wakefield	Wakefield	-	440.00	-
2120	-	60	-	Wakefield	Wakefield	-	800.00	-
2121	-	70	-	Wakefield	Wakefield	160.00	198.40	198.40
2122	-	110	-	Wakefield	Wakefield	480.00	595.20	595.20
2123	-	50	-	Wakefield	Durham	64.00	79.36	-
2124	-	100	-	Wakefield	Durham	64.00	79.36	158.72
2125	-	55	-	Wakefield	Wakefield	26.00	32.24	32.24
2126	-	14	-	Wakefield	Wakefield	190.00	235.60	235.60
2127	-	33	-	Wakefield	Wakefield	140.00	173.60	-
2128	-	40	-	Wakefield	Wakefield	80.00	99.20	272.80
2201	-	70	-	Wakefield	Wakefield	380.00	471.20	471.20
2202	-	67	-	Wakefield	Wakefield	390.00	483.60	483.60
2203	-	67	-	Wakefield	Wakefield	448.00	555.52	555.52
2204	-	120	-	Wakefield	Wakefield	600.00	744.00	744.00
2205	-	50	-	Wakefield	Wakefield	150.00	186.00	186.00
2206	-	100	-	Wakefield	Stratham	200.00	248.00	248.00
2207	-	92	-	Wakefield	Wakefield	460.00	570.40	-
2208	-	50	-	Wakefield	Wakefield	50.00	62.00	632.40
2209	-	25	-	Wakefield	Wakefield	30.00	37.20	-
2210	-	50	-	Wakefield	Wakefield	60.00	74.40	111.60
2211	-	5	-	Wakefield	Wakefield	55.00	68.20	68.20
2212	-	84	-	Wakefield	Wakefield	470.00	582.80	582.80
2213	-	50	-	Wakefield	Wakefield	130.00	161.20	161.20
2214	-	200	-	Wakefield	Wakefield	1200.00	1488.00	1488.00
2215	-	100	-	Wakefield	Wakefield	350.00	434.00	434.00
2216	-	50	-	Wakefield	Wakefield	310.00	384.40	384.40

1798 DIRECT TAX

Pg/No	Occupant Surname	Occupant First Name	Owner Surname	Owner First Name	Dwg #	Val $	Expt Acr
2217	Watson	Stephen	Watson	Stephen	-	-	-
2218	Weeks	John	Weeks	John	-	-	-
2219	Welch	Jacob	Welch	Jacob	-	-	-
2220	Unimproved	-	Welch	Jacob	-	-	-
2221	Wentworth	Elias	Wentworth	Elias	-	-	-
2222	Wentworth	John	Wentworth	John	1	30	-
2223	Wentworth	Sylvanus	Wentworth	Sylvanus	1	5	-
2224	Wiggin	Henry	Wiggin	Henry	-	-	-
2225	Wiggin	Jacob	Wiggin	Jacob	1	20	-
2226	Wiggin	Simeon	Wiggin	Simeon	1	20	-
2301	Wiggin	Isaiah	Wiggin	Isaiah	1	64	-
2302	Unimproved	-	Wiggin	Isaiah	-	-	-
2303	Wingate	John	Wingate	John	-	-	-
2304	Witham	John	Witham	John	1	-	-
2305	Young	James	Young	James	-	-	-
2306	Unimproved	-	Young	James	-	-	-
2307	Wentworth	Spencer	Young	Joseph	-	-	-
2308	Unimproved	-	Unknown	-	-	-	-
2309	Unimproved	-	Unknown	-	-	-	-
2310	Unimproved	-	Unknown	-	-	-	-
2311	Unimproved	-	Unknown	-	-	-	-
2312	Unimproved	-	Unknown	-	-	-	-
2313	Unimproved	-	Unknown	-	-	-	-
2314	Unimproved	-	Unknown	-	-	-	-
2315	Unimproved	-	Unknown	-	-	-	-
2316	Unimproved	-	Unknown	-	-	-	-
2317	Unimproved	-	Unknown	-	-	-	-
2318	Unimproved	-	Unknown	-	-	-	-
2319	Unimproved	-	Unknown	-	-	-	-
2320	Unimproved	-	Unknown	-	-	-	-
2321	Unimproved	-	Unknown	-	-	-	-
2322	Unimproved	-	Unknown	-	-	-	-
2323	Unimproved	-	Unknown	-	-	-	-
2324	Unimproved	-	Unknown	-	-	-	-
2325	Unimproved	-	Unknown	-	-	-	-
2326	Unimproved	-	Unknown	-	-	-	-
2401	Unimproved	-	Unknown	-	-	-	-
2402	Unimproved	-	Unknown	-	-	-	-
2403	Unimproved	-	Unknown	-	-	-	-
2404	Unimproved	-	Unknown	-	-	-	-
2405	Unimproved	-	Unknown	-	-	-	-
2406	Unimproved	-	Unknown	-	-	-	-
2407	Unimproved	-	Unknown	-	-	-	-
2408	Unimproved	-	Unknown	-	-	-	-
2409	Unimproved	-	Unknown	-	-	-	-
2410	Unimproved	-	Unknown	-	-	-	-
2411	Unimproved	-	Unknown	-	-	-	-

NEW HAMPSHIRE DISTRICT 13

Pg/No	Ext Per	Acr	Per	Property Location	Residence of Owner	Value $	Eq. Val $	Total $
2217	-	140	-	Wakefield	Wakefield	850.00	1054.00	1054.00
2218	-	75	-	Wakefield	Wakefield	375.00	465.00	465.00
2219	-	105	-	Wakefield	Wakefield	465.00	576.60	-
2220	-	70	-	Wakefield	Wakefield	30.00	37.20	613.80
2221	-	60	-	Wakefield	Wakefield	120.00	148.80	148.80
2222	-	60	-	Wakefield	Wakefield	200.00	248.00	248.00
2223	-	100	-	Wakefield	Wakefield	340.00	421.60	421.60
2224	-	270	-	Wakefield	Wakefield	1350.00	1674.00	1674.00
2225	-	100	-	Wakefield	Wakefield	350.00	434.00	434.00
2226	-	75	-	Wakefield	Wakefield	315.00	390.60	390.60
2301	-	100	-	Wakefield	Wakefield	600.00	744.00	-
2302	-	16	-	Wakefield	Wakefield	64.00	79.36	823.36
2303	-	170	-	Wakefield	Wakefield	1200.00	1488.00	1488.00
2304	-	20	-	Wakefield	Wakefield	50.00	62.00	62.00
2305	-	156	-	Wakefield	Wakefield	600.00	744.00	-
2306	-	100	-	Wakefield	Wakefield	200.00	248.00	992.00
2307	-	70	-	Wakefield	NewMarket	210.00	260.40	260.40
2308	-	100	-	Wakefield	Wakefield	42.00	52.08	52.08
2309	-	67	-	Wakefield	Wakefield	92.00	114.08	114.08
2310	-	100	-	Wakefield	Wakefield	84.00	104.16	104.16
2311	-	100	-	Wakefield	Wakefield	42.00	52.08	52.08
2312	-	100	-	Wakefield	Wakefield	42.00	52.08	52.08
2313	-	100	-	Wakefield	Wakefield	106.00	131.44	131.44
2314	-	100	-	Wakefield	Wakefield	106.00	131.44	131.44
2315	-	55	-	Wakefield	Wakefield	32.00	39.68	39.68
2316	-	55	-	Wakefield	Wakefield	42.00	52.08	52.08
2317	-	50	-	Wakefield	Wakefield	42.00	52.08	52.08
2318	-	100	-	Wakefield	Wakefield	42.00	52.08	52.08
2319	-	55	-	Wakefield	Wakefield	84.00	104.16	104.16
2320	-	79	-	Wakefield	Wakefield	42.00	52.08	52.08
2321	-	100	-	Wakefield	Wakefield	42.00	52.08	52.08
2322	-	100	-	Wakefield	Wakefield	42.00	52.08	52.08
2323	-	100	-	Wakefield	Wakefield	42.00	52.08	52.08
2324	-	100	-	Wakefield	Wakefield	84.00	104.16	104.16
2325	-	-	-	Wakefield	Wakefield	210.00	260.40	260.40
2326	-	100	-	Wakefield	Wakefield	42.00	52.08	52.08
2401	-	100	-	Wakefield	Wakefield	84.00	104.16	104.16
2402	-	100	-	Wakefield	Wakefield	92.00	114.08	114.08
2403	-	100	-	Wakefield	Wakefield	92.00	114.08	114.08
2404	-	100	-	Wakefield	Wakefield	84.00	104.16	104.16
2405	-	100	-	Wakefield	Wakefield	42.00	52.08	52.08
2406	-	100	-	Wakefield	Wakefield	42.00	52.08	52.08
2407	-	100	-	Wakefield	Wakefield	42.00	52.08	52.08
2408	-	28	-	Wakefield	Wakefield	30.00	37.20	37.20
2409	-	100	-	Wakefield	Wakefield	84.00	104.16	104.16
2410	-	100	-	Wakefield	Wakefield	42.00	52.08	52.08
2411	-	100	-	Wakefield	Wakefield	92.00	114.08	114.08

1798 DIRECT TAX

Pg/No	Occupant Surname	Occupant First Name	Owner Surname	Owner First Name	Dwg #	Val $	Expt Acr
2412	Unimproved	-	Unknown	-	-	-	-
2413	Unimproved	-	Unknown	-	-	-	-
2414	Unimproved	-	Unknown	-	-	-	-
2415	Buzzell	Jonathan	Buzzell	Jonathan	1	50	-
2416	Buzzell	Jonathan	Buzzell	Jonathan	-	-	-
2417	Buzzell	William	Buzzell	William	1	70	-
2418	Buzzell	William, Jr.	Buzzell	William, Jr.	-	-	-
2419	Place	Moses	Chesley	Benjamin	-	-	-
2420	Chesley	Shadrach	Chesley	Shadrach	1	10	-
2421	Clark	Samuel	Clark	Samuel	1	5	-
2422	Colbath	Benning	Colbath	Benning	1	10	-
2423	Colbath	George	Colbath	George	1	10	-
2424	Colbath	Samuel	Colbath	Samuel	-	-	-
2425	-	-	Colomy	John	-	-	-
2426	-	-	Colomy	Daniel	-	-	-
2501	Cook	Joseph	Cook	Joseph	-	-	-
2502	Cook	Joseph	Cook	Joseph	-	-	-
2503	Cook	Robert	Cook	Robert	-	-	-
2504	Cook	Robert	Cook	Robert	-	-	-
2505	Davis	John	Davis	John	-	-	-
2506	Davis	John	Davis	John	-	-	-
2507	Drew	Aaron	Drew	Aaron	-	-	-
2508	Durgan	Josiah	Durgan	Josiah	-	-	-
2509	Ellis	Ephraim	Ellis	Ephraim	1	3	-
2510	Ellis	Joseph	Ellis	Joseph	1	90	-
2511	Unimproved	-	Footman	Thomas	-	-	-
2512	Frost	Nicholas	Frost	Nicholas	1	5	-
2513	Frost	Samuel	Frost	Samuel	-	-	-
2514	Frost	Samuel	Frost	Samuel	-	-	-
2515	Frost	Samuel	Frost	Samuel	1	-	-
2516	Unimproved	-	Gage	Jonathan	-	-	-
2517	Garlin	Thomas	Garlin	Thomas	1	99	-
2518	Garlin	Thomas	Garlin	Thomas	-	-	-
2519	Garlin	Thomas	Garlin	Thomas	-	-	-
2520	Gerrish	James	Gerrish	James	-	-	-
2521	Gerrish	Paul	Gerrish	Paul	1	10	-
2522	Hanson	Timothy	Hanson	Timothy	1	1	-
2523	Hardy	Jonathan	Hardy	Jonathan	1	5	-
2524	Heix	John	Heix	John	1	5	-
2525	Hiner	John H.	Hiner	John H.	-	-	-
2526	Hiner	John H.	Hiner	John H.	-	-	-
2527	Hiner	John H.	Hiner	John H.	-	-	-
2601	Unimproved	-	Hardy	Robert	-	-	-
2602	Unimproved	-	Hodgdon	Caleb	-	-	-
2603	Horn	Jethro	Horn	Jethro	1	20	-
2604	Unimproved	-	Jaffrey	George	-	-	-
2605	Johnson	Gideon	Johnson	Gideon	1	3	-

NEW HAMPSHIRE DISTRICT 13

Pg/No	Ext Per	Acr	Per	Property Location	Residence of Owner	Value $	Eq. Val $	Total $
2412	-	100	-	Wakefield	Wakefield	64.00	79.36	79.36
2413	-	100	-	Wakefield	Wakefield	94.00	116.56	116.56
2414	-	100	-	Wakefield	Wakefield	42.00	52.08	52.08
2415	-	188	-	Middleton	Middleton	504.00	624.96	-
2416	-	50	-	Middleton	Middleton	70.00	86.80	711.76
2417	-	100	-	Middleton	Middleton	470.00	582.80	-
2418	-	100	-	Middleton	Middleton	125.00	155.00	-
2419	-	50	-	Middleton	Durham	150.00	186.00	-
2420	-	300	-	Middleton	Middleton	540.00	669.60	-
2421	-	50	-	Middleton	Middleton	120.00	148.80	-
2422	-	53	-	Middleton	Middleton	190.00	235.60	-
2423	-	50	-	Middleton	Middleton	110.00	136.40	-
2424	-	50	-	Middleton	Middleton	100.00	124.00	-
2425	-	55	-	Middleton	New Durham	147.50	182.90	-
2426	-	50	-	Middleton	New Durham	100.00	124.00	-
2501	-	75	-	Middleton	Middleton	454.00	562.96	-
2502	-	81	-	Middleton	Middleton	162.00	200.88	763.84
2503	-	200	-	Middleton	Middleton	500.00	620.00	-
2504	-	25	-	Middleton	Middleton	50.00	62.00	682.00
2505	-	150	-	Middleton	Middleton	300.00	372.00	-
2506	-	150	-	Middleton	Middleton	250.00	310.00	682.00
2507	-	100	-	Middleton	Middleton	100.00	124.00	124.00
2508	-	30	-	Middleton	Middleton	90.00	111.60	111.60
2509	-	100	-	Middleton	Middleton	100.00	124.00	124.00
2510	-	150	-	Middleton	Middleton	550.00	682.00	682.00
2511	-	50	-	Middleton	Dover	100.00	124.00	124.00
2512	-	50	-	Middleton	Middleton	130.00	161.20	161.20
2513	-	50	-	Middleton	Middleton	200.00	248.00	-
2514	-	50	-	Middleton	Middleton	30.00	37.20	-
2515	-	20	-	Middleton	Middleton	100.00	124.00	409.20
2516	-	100	-	Middleton	Dover	100.00	124.00	124.00
2517	-	100	-	Middleton	Middleton	420.00	520.80	-
2518	-	50	-	Middleton	Middleton	170.00	210.80	-
2519	-	3	-	Middleton	Middleton	5.00	6.20	737.80
2520	-	56	-	Middleton	Middleton	205.00	254.20	254.20
2521	-	20	-	Middleton	Middleton	60.00	74.40	74.40
2522	-	150	-	Middleton	Middleton	300.00	372.00	372.00
2523	-	50	-	Middleton	Middleton	160.00	198.40	198.40
2524	-	100	-	Middleton	Middleton	330.00	409.20	409.20
2525	-	50	-	Middleton	Middleton	150.00	186.00	-
2526	-	100	-	Middleton	Middleton	120.00	148.80	-
2527	-	85	-	Middleton	Middleton	44.00	54.56	389.36
2601	-	94	-	Middleton	Wakefield	50.00	62.00	62.00
2602	-	100	-	Middleton	Dover	200.00	248.00	248.00
2603	-	110	-	Middleton	Middleton	180.00	223.20	223.20
2604	-	100	-	Middleton	Portsmouth	100.00	124.00	124.00
2605	-	100	-	Middleton	Middleton	203.00	251.72	251.72

1798 DIRECT TAX

Pg/No	Occupant Surname	Occupant First Name	Owner Surname	Owner First Name	Dwg #	Val $	Expt Acr
2606	Johnson	Samuel	Johnson	Samuel	1	30	-
2607	Kennison	Chase	Kennison	Chase	-	-	-
2608	Kennison	John	Kennison	John	1	10	-
2609	Kimball	Enoch	Kimball	Enoch	1	5	-
2610	Leighton	David	Leighton	David	1	30	-
2611	Moulton	Robert	Moulton	Robert	1	3	-
2612	Unimproved	-	Palmer	Jonathan	-	-	-
2613	Unimproved	-	Palmer	Jonathan	-	-	-
2614	Unimproved	-	Palmer	Jonathan	-	-	-
2615	Unimproved	-	Palmer	Jonathan	-	-	-
2616	Unimproved	-	Palmer	Jonathan	-	-	-
2617	Unimproved	-	Palmer	Jonathan	-	-	-
2618	Unimproved	-	Palmer	Jonathan	-	-	-
2619	Palmer	James	Palmer	James	-	-	-
2620	Unimproved	-	Penhallow	John	-	-	-
2621	Unimproved	-	Piper	Asa	-	-	-
2622	Unimproved	-	Piper	Asa	-	-	-
2623	Unimproved	-	Piper	Asa	-	-	-
2624	Perkins	Solomon	Perkins	Solomon	1	70	-
2625	Perkins	Solomon	Perkins	Solomon	-	-	-
2626	Pike	Henry	Pike	Henry	-	-	-
2701	Pike	Jacob	Pike	Jacob	-	-	-
2702	Pike	Jacob, Jr.	Pike	Jacob, Jr.	1	8	-
2703	Pottle	Simon	Pottle	Simon	1	4	-
2704	Richards	Tristram	Richards	Tristram	1	5	-
2705	Roberts	George	Roberts	George	-	-	-
2706	Roberts	George	Roberts	George	-	-	-
2707	Roberts	George	Roberts	George	-	-	-
2708	Runnels	Ebenezer	Runnels	Ebenezer	-	-	-
2709	Woodman	Arch's	Smith	Ebenezer	1	60	-
2710	Stanton	Isaac	Stanton	Isaac	1	55	-
2711	Stevens	David	Stevens	David	1	98	-
2712	-	-	Tash	John	1	90	-
2713	-	-	Tash	John	-	-	-
2714	-	-	Tash	John	-	-	-
2715	-	-	Tash	John	-	-	-
2716	-	-	Tash	John	-	-	-
2717	-	-	Tash	John	-	-	-
2718	-	-	Tash	John	-	-	-
2719	-	-	Tash	John	-	-	-
2720	-	-	Tash	John	-	-	-
2721	-	-	Tash	John	-	-	-
2722	-	-	Tash	John	-	-	-
2723	Thomas	James	Thomas	James	1	10	-
2724	-	-	Thomas	James	-	-	-
2725	Trickey	Ephraim	Trickey	Ephraim	-	-	-

NEW HAMPSHIRE DISTRICT 13

Pg/No	Ext Per	Acr	Per	Property Location	Residence of Owner	Value $	Eq. Val $	Total $
2606	-	100	-	Middleton	Middleton	280.00	347.20	347.20
2607	-	50	-	Middleton	Middleton	150.00	186.00	186.00
2608	-	100	-	Middleton	Middleton	340.00	421.60	421.60
2609	-	100	-	Middleton	Middleton	155.00	192.20	192.20
2610	-	50	-	Middleton	Middleton	180.00	223.20	223.20
2611	-	50	-	Middleton	Middleton	153.00	189.72	189.72
2612	-	100	-	Middleton	Wakefield	100.00	124.00	-
2613	-	100	-	Middleton	Wakefield	100.00	124.00	-
2614	-	100	-	Middleton	Wakefield	100.00	124.00	-
2615	-	100	-	Middleton	Wakefield	100.00	124.00	-
2616	-	70	-	Middleton	Wakefield	70.00	86.80	-
2617	-	140	-	Middleton	Wakefield	140.00	173.60	-
2618	-	50	-	Middleton	Wakefield	50.00	62.00	818.40
2619	-	46	-	Middleton	Middleton	140.00	173.60	173.60
2620	-	100	-	Middleton	Portsmouth	150.00	186.00	186.00
2621	-	50	-	Middleton	Wakefield	75.00	93.00	-
2622	-	100	-	Middleton	Wakefield	162.50	201.50	-
2623	-	100	-	Middleton	Wakefield	162.50	201.50	496.00
2624	-	160	-	Middleton	Middleton	385.00	477.40	-
2625	-	50	-	Middleton	Middleton	25.00	31.00	508.40
2626	-	100	-	Middleton	Middleton	300.00	372.00	372.00
2701	-	175	-	Middleton	Middleton	600.00	744.00	744.00
2702	-	80	-	Middleton	Middleton	240.00	297.60	297.60
2703	-	2	-	Middleton	Middleton	25.00	31.00	31.00
2704	-	69	-	Middleton	Middleton	130.00	161.20	161.20
2705	-	50	-	Middleton	Middleton	50.00	62.00	-
2706	-	94	-	Middleton	Middleton	47.00	58.28	-
2707	-	50	-	Middleton	Middleton	25.00	31.00	151.28
2708	-	30	-	Middleton	Middleton	60.00	74.40	74.40
2709	-	50	-	Middleton	Durham	300.00	372.00	372.00
2710	-	100	-	Middleton	Middleton	400.00	496.00	496.00
2711	-	100	-	Middleton	Middleton	390.00	483.60	483.60
2712	-	100	-	Middleton	New Market	630.00	781.20	-
2713	-	97	-	Middleton	New Market	194.00	240.56	-
2714	-	100	-	Middleton	New Market	200.00	248.00	-
2715	-	100	-	Middleton	New Market	200.00	248.00	-
2716	-	100	-	Middleton	New Market	200.00	248.00	-
2717	-	100	-	Middleton	New Market	200.00	248.00	-
2718	-	100	-	Middleton	New Market	200.00	248.00	-
2719	-	100	-	Middleton	New Market	200.00	248.00	-
2720	-	100	-	Middleton	New Market	200.00	248.00	-
2721	-	100	-	Middleton	New Market	200.00	248.00	-
2722	-	100	-	Middleton	New Market	300.00	372.00	3377.76
2723	-	60	-	Middleton	Middleton	300.00	372.00	-
2724	-	70	-	Middleton	Middleton	200.00	248.00	620.00
2725	-	50	-	Middleton	Middleton	50.00	62.00	62.00

1798 DIRECT TAX

Pg/No	Occupant Surname	Occupant First Name	Owner Surname	Owner First Name	Dwg #	Val $	Expt Acr
2726	Twambly	Paul	Twambly	Paul	1	5	-
2801	Twombly	William	Twombly	William	-	-	-
2802	Whitehouse	Daniel	Whitehouse	Daniel	1	15	-
2803	Whitehouse	John	Whitehouse	John	1	90	-
2804	Whitehouse	Nathaniel	Whitehouse	Nathaniel	1	10	-
2805	Whitehouse	Paul	Whitehouse	Paul	1	70	-
2806	-	-	Whitehouse	Paul	-	-	-
2807	Whitehouse	Silas	Whitehouse	Silas	1	20	-
2808	Wingate	Daniel	Wingate	Daniel	-	-	-
2809	-	-	Wingate	Daniel	-	-	-
2810	York	Benjamin	York	Benjamin	-	-	-
2811	York	John	York	John	1	10	-
2812	York	Josiah	York	Josiah	1	90	-
2813	York	Josiah, Jr.	York	Josiah, Jr.	1	15	-
2814	York	Thomas	York	Thomas	1	5	-
2815	Unimproved	-	Unknown	-	-	-	-
2816	Unimproved	-	Unknown	-	-	-	-
2817	Unimproved	-	Unknown	-	-	-	-
2818	Unimproved	-	Unknown	-	-	-	-
2819	Unimproved	-	Unknown	-	-	-	-
2820	Unimproved	-	Unknown	-	-	-	-
2821	Unimproved	-	Unknown	-	-	-	-
2822	Unimproved	-	Unknown	-	-	-	-
2823	Unimproved	-	Unknown	-	-	-	-
2824	Unimproved	-	Unknown	-	-	-	-
2825	Unimproved	-	Unknown	-	-	-	-
2826	Unimproved	-	Unknown	-	-	-	-
2901	Unimproved	-	Unknown	-	-	-	-
2902	Unimproved	-	Unknown	-	-	-	-
2903	Unimproved	-	Unknown	-	-	-	-
2904	Unimproved	-	Unknown	-	-	-	-
2905	Allard	Benjamin	Allard	Benjamin	-	-	-
2906	Baker	Charles	Baker	Charles	1	20	-
2907	Baker	Thomas	Baker	Thomas	-	-	-
2908	-	-	Bennett	Eleazer	-	-	-
2909	Boody	Aaron	Boody	Aaron	-	-	-
2910	Brown	Joseph	Brown	Joseph	-	-	-
2911	Burk	James	Burk	James	-	-	-
2912	Chamberlain	John	Chamberlain	John	1	30	-
2913	Calder	Robert	Calder	Robert	-	-	-
2914	Cate	Neal	Cate	Neal	1	25	-
2915	Chamberlain	James	Chamberlain	James	-	-	-
2916	Chamberlain	Thomas	Chamberlain	Thomas	-	-	-
2917	Chamberlain	William	Chamberlain	William	-	-	-
2918	Chappotin	Leon	Chappotin	Leon	-	-	-
2919	Clay	Benjamin	Clay	Benjamin	-	-	-
2920	Clay	Jonathan	Clay	Jonathan	1	20	-

NEW HAMPSHIRE DISTRICT 13

Pg/No	Ext Per	Acr	Per	Property Location	Residence of Owner	Value $	Eq. Val $	Total $
2726	-	50	-	Middleton	Middleton	105.00	130.20	130.20
2801	-	50	-	Middleton	Middleton	60.00	74.40	74.40
2802	-	90	-	Middleton	Middleton	115.00	142.60	142.60
2803	-	100	-	Middleton	Middleton	390.00	483.60	483.60
2804	-	30	-	Middleton	Middleton	70.00	86.80	86.80
2805	-	50	-	Middleton	Middleton	310.00	384.40	-
2806	-	50	-	Middleton	Middleton	30.00	37.20	421.60
2807	-	2	-	Middleton	Middleton	70.00	86.80	86.80
2808	-	100	-	Middleton	Middleton	150.00	186.00	-
2809	-	40	-	Middleton	Middleton	150.00	186.00	372.00
2810	-	50	-	Middleton	Middleton	120.00	148.80	148.80
2811	-	50	-	Middleton	Middleton	200.00	248.00	248.00
2812	-	150	-	Middleton	Middleton	400.00	496.00	496.00
2813	-	50	-	Middleton	Middleton	130.00	161.20	161.20
2814	-	50	-	Middleton	Middleton	130.00	161.20	161.20
2815	-	6	-	Middleton	Middleton	3.00	3.72	3.72
2816	-	50	-	Middleton	Middleton	25.00	31.00	31.00
2817	-	100	-	Middleton	Middleton	50.00	62.00	62.00
2818	-	100	-	Middleton	Middleton	50.00	62.00	62.00
2819	-	100	-	Middleton	Middleton	50.00	62.00	62.00
2820	-	50	-	Middleton	Middleton	50.00	62.00	62.00
2821	-	100	-	Middleton	Middleton	50.00	62.00	62.00
2822	-	100	-	Middleton	Middleton	50.00	62.00	62.00
2823	-	100	-	Middleton	Middleton	50.00	62.00	62.00
2824	-	100	-	Middleton	Middleton	50.00	62.00	62.00
2825	-	100	-	Middleton	Middleton	50.00	62.00	62.00
2826	-	50	-	Middleton	Middleton	50.00	62.00	62.00
2901	-	15	-	Middleton	Middleton	15.00	18.60	18.60
2902	-	100	-	Middleton	Middleton	50.00	62.00	62.00
2903	-	100	-	Middleton	Middleton	50.00	62.00	62.00
2904	-	50	-	Middleton	Middleton	50.00	62.00	62.00
2905	-	70	-	Brookfield	Brookfield	166.00	205.84	205.84
2906	-	140	-	Brookfield	Brookfield	200.00	248.00	248.00
2907	-	210	-	Brookfield	Brookfield	565.00	700.60	760.00
2908	-	140	-	Brookfield	Durham	200.00	248.00	248.00
2909	-	140	-	Brookfield	Brookfield	130.00	161.20	161.20
2910	-	50	-	Brookfield	Brookfield	100.00	124.00	124.00
2911	-	50	-	Brookfield	Brookfield	50.00	62.00	62.00
2912	-	142	-	Brookfield	Brookfield	750.00	930.00	930.00
2913	-	180	-	Brookfield	Brookfield	770.00	954.80	954.80
2914	-	113	-	Brookfield	Brookfield	590.00	731.60	731.60
2915	-	200	-	Brookfield	Brookfield	900.00	1116.00	1116.00
2916	-	389	-	Brookfield	Brookfield	1400.00	1736.00	1736.00
2917	-	122	-	Brookfield	Brookfield	830.00	1029.20	1029.20
2918	-	11	-	Brookfield	Brookfield	66.00	81.84	81.84
2919	-	63	-	Brookfield	Brookfield	476.00	590.24	590.24
2920	-	47	-	Brookfield	Brookfield	302.00	374.48	374.48

1798 DIRECT TAX

Pg/No	Occupant Surname	Occupant First Name	Owner Surname	Owner First Name	Dwg #	Val $	Expt Acr
2921	Coleman	Mary	Coleman	Mary	-	-	-
2922	Unimproved	-	Copp	David	-	-	-
2923	Daniels	Reuben	Daniels	Reuben	-	-	-
2924	Daniels	Obadiah	Daniels	Obadiah	-	-	-
2925	Deeling	Jonathan	Deeling	Jonathan	1	20	-
2926	Deeling	Samuel	Deeling	Samuel	1	15	-
3001	Drew	Andrew	Drew	Andrew	-	-	-
3002	Drew	Joseph	Drew	Joseph	-	-	-
3003	Durgan	John	Durgan	John	-	-	-
3004	Edgerly	James	Edgerly	James	1	15	-
3005	Fernald	John	Fernald	John	-	-	-
3006	Unimproved	-	Gage	Jonathan	-	-	-
3007	Giles	Charles	Giles	Charles	-	-	-
3008	Giles	John	Giles	John	1	25	-
3009	Guppy	Joshua	Guppy	Joshua	-	-	-
3010	Unimproved	-	Gilman	John	-	-	-
3011	Hanson	Reuben	Hanson	Reuben	1	30	-
3012	Hanson	Richard	Hanson	Richard	-	-	-
3013	Hanson	Tobias	Hanson	Tobias	-	-	-
3014	Hodge	Hiram	Hacket	James	-	-	-
3015	Unimproved	-	Hall	Samuel	-	-	-
3016	Horn	Edmund	Horn	Edmund	1	15	-
3017	Horn	Jacob	Horn	Jacob	1	15	-
3018	Unimproved	-	Horn	Daniel	-	-	-
3019	Johnson	Phineas	Johnson	Phineas	-	-	-
3020	Johnson	Timothy	Johnson	Timothy	-	-	-
3021	Unimproved	-	Jaffrey	George	-	-	-
3022	Kent	William	Kent	William	1	30	-
3023	Kennison	Thomas	Kennison	Thomas	1	40	-
3024	Kennison	Thomas	Kennison	Thomas	-	-	-
3025	Kennison	Waldron	Kennison	Waldron	-	-	-
3026	Unimproved	-	Libby	Reuben	-	-	-
3101	Lyford	Robert	Lyford	Robert	1	20	-
3102	Lyford	Stephen	Lyford	Stephen	-	-	-
3103	Martin	John	Martin	John	-	-	-
3104	Martin	Timothy	Martin	Timothy	1	25	-
3105	Palmer	John	Palmer	John	1	20	-
3106	Perkins	John	Perkins	John	1	20	-
3107	Perkins	Moses	Perkins	Moses	1	15	-
3108	Perkins	Moses, Jr.	Perkins	Moses, Jr.	-	-	-
3109	-	-	Perkins	Moses, Jr.	-	-	-
3110	Pike	Robert	Pike	Robert	1	20	-
3111	Ricker	Joseph	Ricker	Joseph	1	20	-
3112	Unimproved	-	Richards	Bartholomew	-	-	-
3113	Robinson	Tristram H.	Robinson	Tristram H.	-	-	-
3114	Robinson	Walter	Robinson	Walter	1	30	-
3115	Sanborn	Ezekiel	Sanborn	Ezekiel	-	-	-

NEW HAMPSHIRE DISTRICT 13

Pg/No	Ext Per	Acr	Per	Property Location	Residence of Owner	Value $	Eq. Val $	Total $
2921	-	400	-	Brookfield	Brookfield	1760.00	2182.40	2182.40
2922	-	35	-	Brookfield	Wakefield	51.00	63.24	63.24
2923	-	50	-	Brookfield	Brookfield	120.00	148.80	148.80
2924	-	50	-	Brookfield	Brookfield	100.00	124.00	124.00
2925	-	40	-	Brookfield	Brookfield	60.00	74.40	74.40
2926	-	100	-	Brookfield	Brookfield	115.00	142.60	142.60
3001	-	60	-	Brookfield	Brookfield	470.00	582.80	582.80
3002	-	20	-	Brookfield	Brookfield	20.00	24.80	24.80
3003	-	140	-	Brookfield	Brookfield	300.00	372.00	372.00
3004	-	95	-	Brookfield	Brookfield	110.00	136.40	136.40
3005	-	130	-	Brookfield	Brookfield	635.00	787.40	787.40
3006	-	100	-	Brookfield	Dover	100.00	124.00	124.00
3007	-	56	-	Brookfield	Brookfield	200.00	248.00	248.00
3008	-	50	-	Brookfield	Brookfield	170.00	210.80	210.80
3009	-	140	-	Brookfield	Brookfield	600.00	744.00	744.00
3010	-	20	-	Brookfield	Wakefield	60.00	74.40	74.40
3011	-	70	-	Brookfield	Brookfield	195.00	241.80	241.80
3012	-	200	-	Brookfield	Brookfield	1115.00	1382.60	1382.60
3013	-	245	-	Brookfield	Brookfield	400.00	496.00	496.00
3014	-	375	-	Brookfield	Piscatuqua Isle	1866.00	2313.84	2313.84
3015	-	130	-	Brookfield	Wakefield	200.00	248.00	248.00
3016	-	55	-	Brookfield	Brookfield	215.00	266.60	266.60
3017	-	54	-	Brookfield	Brookfield	145.00	179.80	179.80
3018	-	42	-	Brookfield	Wakefield	84.00	104.16	104.16
3019	-	158	-	Brookfield	Brookfield	666.00	825.84	825.84
3020	-	199	-	Brookfield	Brookfield	1040.00	1289.60	1289.60
3021	-	130	-	Brookfield	Portsmouth	168.00	208.32	208.32
3022	-	100	-	Brookfield	Brookfield	530.00	657.20	657.20
3023	-	55	-	Brookfield	Brookfield	317.00	391.84	-
3024	-	50	-	Brookfield	Brookfield	100.00	124.00	515.84
3025	-	170	-	Brookfield	Brookfield	900.00	1116.00	1116.00
3026	-	70	-	Brookfield	Wolfeboro	25.00	31.00	31.00
3101	-	86	-	Brookfield	Brookfield	192.00	238.08	238.08
3102	-	124	-	Brookfield	Brookfield	665.00	824.60	824.60
3103	-	100	-	Brookfield	Brookfield	370.00	458.80	458.80
3104	-	180	-	Brookfield	Brookfield	810.00	1004.40	1004.40
3105	-	50	-	Brookfield	Brookfield	295.00	365.80	365.80
3106	-	82	-	Brookfield	Brookfield	254.00	314.96	314.96
3107	-	51	-	Brookfield	Brookfield	294.00	364.56	364.56
3108	-	51	-	Brookfield	Brookfield	102.00	126.48	-
3109	-	30	-	Brookfield	Brookfield	60.00	74.40	200.88
3110	-	160	-	Brookfield	Brookfield	630.00	781.20	781.20
3111	-	50	-	Brookfield	Brookfield	220.00	272.80	272.80
3112	-	100	-	Brookfield	Madbury	100.00	124.00	124.00
3113	-	81	-	Brookfield	Brookfield	273.00	338.52	338.52
3114	-	70	-	Brookfield	Brookfield	270.00	334.80	334.80
3115	-	190	-	Brookfield	Brookfield	825.00	1023.00	1023.00

1798 DIRECT TAX

Pg/No	Occupant Surname	Occupant First Name	Owner Surname	Owner First Name	Dwg #	Val $	Expt Acr
3116	Sayer	Michael	Sayer	Michael	-	-	-
3117	Sherborne	John	Sherborne	John	-	-	-
3118	Stanton	Charles	Stanton	Charles	-	-	-
3119	Stanton	John	Stanton	John	1	36	-
3120	Stodard	Deering	Stodard	Deering	-	-	-
3121	-	-	Tash	John	-	-	-
3122	-	-	Tash	John	-	-	-
3123	-	-	Tash	John	-	-	-
3124	-	-	Tash	John	-	-	-
3125	-	-	Tash	John	-	-	-
3126	-	-	Tash	John	-	-	-
3201	-	-	Tash	John	-	-	-
3202	-	-	Tash	John	-	-	-
3203	Thompson	Moses	Thompson	Moses	-	-	-
3204	Tibbets	Edmund	Tibbets	Edmund	-	-	-
3205	Tibbets	John	Tibbets	John	1	20	-
3206	Tibbets	Samuel	Tibbets	Samuel	-	-	-
3207	Tibbets	Samuel, Jr.	Tibbets	Samuel, Jr.	1	55	-
3208	Tibbets	William	Tibbets	William	1	12	-
3209	-	-	Tibbets	William	-	-	-
3210	Trickey	Benjamin	Trickey	Benjamin	1	20	-
3211	Trickey	William	Trickey	William	1	20	-
3212	Tuttle	Paul	Tuttle	Paul	-	-	-
3213	Watson	David	Watson	David	1	10	-
3214	Watson	Joseph	Watson	Joseph	1	30	-
3215	Watson	Nathan	Watson	Nathan	-	-	-
3216	-	-	Watson	Nathan	-	-	-
3217	-	-	Watson	Nathan	-	-	-
3218	Wentworth	Richard	Wentworth	Richard	1	20	-
3219	Whitehouse	Charles F.	Whitehouse	Charles F.	1	15	-
3220	Whitehouse	Moses	Whitehouse	Moses	-	-	-
3221	-	-	Whitehouse	Moses	-	-	-
3222	-	-	Whitehouse	Moses	-	-	-
3223	Wiggin	Josiah	Wiggin	Josiah	-	-	-
3224	-	-	Wiggin	Josiah	-	-	-
3225	-	-	Wiggin	Josiah	-	-	-
3226	Wiggin	Samuel	Wiggin	Samuel	1	25	-
3301	Wiggin	Thomas	Wiggin	Thomas	1	25	-
3302	Willard	John	Willard	John	1	25	-
3303	Wille	Nathaniel	Wille	Nathaniel	1	18	-
3304	Wille	Moses	Wille	Moses	-	-	-
3305	-	-	Wille	Moses	-	-	-
3306	Wille	Stephen	Wille	Stephen	-	-	-
3307	Unimproved	-	Unknown	-	-	-	-
3308	Unimproved	-	Unknown	-	-	-	-
3309	Unimproved	-	Unknown	-	-	-	-
3310	Unimproved	-	Unknown	-	-	-	-

NEW HAMPSHIRE DISTRICT 13

Pg/No	Ext Per	Acr	Per	Property Location	Residence of Owner	Value $	Eq. Val $	Total $
3116	-	100	-	Brookfield	Brookfield	345.00	427.80	427.80
3117	-	13	-	Brookfield	Brookfield	78.00	96.72	96.72
3118	-	160	-	Brookfield	Brookfield	520.00	644.80	644.80
3119	-	70	-	Brookfield	Brookfield	295.00	365.80	365.80
3120	-	110	-	Brookfield	Brookfield	575.00	713.00	713.00
3121	-	70	-	Brookfield	NewMarket	50.00	62.00	-
3122	-	140	-	Brookfield	Brookfield	65.00	80.60	-
3123	-	140	-	Brookfield	Brookfield	85.00	105.40	-
3124	-	85	-	Brookfield	Brookfield	127.00	157.48	-
3125	-	140	-	Brookfield	Brookfield	100.00	124.00	-
3126	-	140	-	Brookfield	Brookfield	200.00	248.00	777.48
3201	-	140	-	Brookfield	NewMarket	100.00	124.00	-
3202	-	70	-	Brookfield	Brookfield	66.00	81.84	205.84
3203	-	50	-	Brookfield	Brookfield	240.00	297.60	297.60
3204	-	60	-	Brookfield	Brookfield	120.00	148.80	148.80
3205	-	60	-	Brookfield	Brookfield	170.00	210.80	210.80
3206	-	100	-	Brookfield	Brookfield	500.00	620.00	620.00
3207	-	60	-	Brookfield	Brookfield	235.00	291.40	291.40
3208	-	70	-	Brookfield	Brookfield	182.00	225.68	-
3209	-	7	-	Brookfield	Brookfield	21.00	26.04	251.72
3210	-	50	-	Brookfield	Brookfield	100.00	124.00	124.00
3211	-	80	-	Brookfield	Brookfield	320.00	396.80	396.80
3212	-	140	-	Brookfield	Brookfield	280.00	347.20	347.20
3213	-	50	-	Brookfield	Brookfield	260.00	322.40	322.40
3214	-	70	-	Brookfield	Brookfield	170.00	210.80	210.80
3215	-	95	-	Brookfield	Brookfield	618.00	766.32	-
3216	-	45	-	Brookfield	Brookfield	90.00	111.60	-
3217	-	36	-	Brookfield	Brookfield	72.00	89.28	967.20
3218	-	120	-	Brookfield	Brookfield	550.00	682.00	682.00
3219	-	50	-	Brookfield	Brookfield	315.00	390.60	390.60
3220	-	78	-	Brookfield	Brookfield	571.00	708.04	-
3221	-	34	-	Brookfield	Brookfield	85.00	105.40	-
3222	-	52	-	Brookfield	Brookfield	156.00	193.44	1006.88
3223	-	60	-	Brookfield	Brookfield	425.00	527.00	-
3224	-	50	-	Brookfield	Brookfield	125.00	155.00	-
3225	-	20	-	Brookfield	Brookfield	30.00	37.20	719.20
3226	-	100	-	Brookfield	Brookfield	660.00	818.40	818.40
3301	-	70	-	Brookfield	Brookfield	225.00	279.00	279.00
3302	-	-	-	Brookfield	Brookfield	25.00	31.00	31.00
3303	-	70	-	Brookfield	Brookfield	88.00	109.12	109.12
3304	-	70	-	Brookfield	Brookfield	300.00	372.00	-
3305	-	20	-	Brookfield	Brookfield	40.00	49.60	421.60
3306	-	70	-	Brookfield	Brookfield	70.00	86.80	86.80
3307	-	130	-	Brookfield	Brookfield	-	-	-
3308	-	130	-	Brookfield	Brookfield	200.00	248.00	248.00
3309	-	130	-	Brookfield	Brookfield	47.00	58.28	58.28
3310	-	130	-	Brookfield	Brookfield	39.00	48.36	48.36

1798 DIRECT TAX

Pg/No	Occupant Surname	Occupant First Name	Owner Surname	Owner First Name	Dwg #	Val $	Expt Acr
3311	Unimproved	-	Unknown	-	-	-	-
3312	Unimproved	-	Unknown	-	-	-	-
3313	Unimproved	-	Unknown	-	-	-	-
3314	Unimproved	-	Unknown	-	-	-	-
3315	Unimproved	-	Unknown	-	-	-	-
3316	Unimproved	-	Unknown	-	-	-	-
3317	Unimproved	-	Unknown	-	-	-	-
3318	Unimproved	-	Unknown	-	-	-	-
3319	Unimproved	-	Unknown	-	-	-	-
3320	Unimproved	-	Unknown	-	-	-	-
3321	Unimproved	-	Unknown	-	-	-	-
3322	Unimproved	-	Unknown	-	-	-	-
3323	Unimproved	-	Unknown	-	-	-	-
3324	Unimproved	-	Unknown	-	-	-	-
3325	Unimproved	-	Unknown	-	-	-	-
3326	Unimproved	-	Brown	Nathan, Jr.	-	-	-
3401	Unimproved	-	Banfield	Joseph	-	-	-
3402	Baker	John	Baker	John	1	30	-
3403	Bennett	Joseph	Bennett	Joseph	-	-	-
3404	Blazo	John	Blazo	John	-	-	-
3405	Bradbury	Joseph	Bradbury	Joseph	1	12	-
3406	Unimproved	-	Brown	Jacob	-	-	-
3407	Brown	Nathan	Brown	Nathan	1	40	-
3408	Tasker	Ebenezer	Brown	Simon	-	-	-
3409	Bryant	Ithiel	Bryant	Ithiel	1	15	-
3410	Buzzell	John	Buzzell	John	1	30	-
3411	Unimproved	-	Cotton	Edward	-	-	-
3412	Cross	Moses	Cross	Moses	1	10	-
3413	Cooper	Moses	Cooper	Moses	1	10	-
3414	Costellow	Lydia	Costellow	Lydia	-	-	-
3415	Cooper	Levi	Cooper	Levi	-	-	-
3416	Calley	John	Calley	John	-	-	-
3417	Cross	Daniel	Cross	Daniel	-	-	-
3418	Unimproved	-	Cram	Jonathan	-	-	-
3419	-	-	Cram	Jonathan	-	-	-
3420	Dearborn	Asahel	Dearborn	Asahel	-	-	-
3421	Unimproved	-	Dearborn	Asahel	-	-	-
3422	Unimproved	-	Dearborn	Asahel	-	-	-
3423	Dearborn	Benjamin	Dearborn	Benjamin	1	10	-
3424	Unimproved	-	Dearborn	John	-	-	-
3425	Doe	John	Doe	John	1	30	-
3426	Doe	Joseph	Doe	Joseph	1	40	-
3501	Dearborn	John S.	Dearborn	John S.	-	-	-
3502	Unimproved	-	Dearborn	John S.	-	-	-
3503	Unimproved	-	Dearborn	John S.	-	-	-
3504	Unimproved	-	Dearborn	John S.	-	-	-
3505	Unimproved	-	Dearborn	John S.	-	-	-

NEW HAMPSHIRE DISTRICT 13

Pg/No	Ext Per	Acr	Per	Property Location	Residence of Owner	Value $	Eq. Val $	Total $
3311	-	90	-	Brookfield	Brookfield	135.00	167.40	167.40
3312	-	70	-	Brookfield	Brookfield	100.00	124.00	124.00
3313	-	100	-	Brookfield	Brookfield	35.00	43.40	43.40
3314	-	130	-	Brookfield	Brookfield	168.00	208.32	208.32
3315	-	45	-	Brookfield	Brookfield	50.00	62.00	62.00
3316	-	130	-	Brookfield	Brookfield	33.00	40.92	40.92
3317	-	70	-	Brookfield	Brookfield	66.00	81.84	81.84
3318	-	130	-	Brookfield	Brookfield	39.00	48.36	48.36
3319	-	130	-	Brookfield	Brookfield	33.00	40.92	40.92
3320	-	130	-	Brookfield	Brookfield	93.00	115.32	115.32
3321	-	130	-	Brookfield	Brookfield	135.00	167.40	167.40
3322	-	130	-	Brookfield	Brookfield	113.00	140.12	140.12
3323	-	130	-	Brookfield	Brookfield	66.00	81.84	81.84
3324	-	130	-	Brookfield	Brookfield	33.00	40.92	40.92
3325	-	90	-	Brookfield	Brookfield	100.00	124.00	124.00
3326	-	200	-	Effingham	Hampton Falls	300.00	372.00	372.00
3401	-	200	-	Effingham	Eaton	200.00	248.00	248.00
3402	-	100	-	Effingham	Effingham	380.00	471.20	471.20
3403	-	50	-	Effingham	Effingham	125.00	155.00	155.00
3404	-	20	-	Effingham	Effingham	40.00	49.60	49.60
3405	-	50	-	Effingham	Effingham	112.00	138.88	138.88
3406	-	200	-	Effingham	East Kingston	100.00	124.00	124.00
3407	-	32	-	Effingham	Effingham	156.00	193.44	193.44
3408	-	240	-	Effingham	North Hampton	770.00	954.80	954.80
3409	-	60	-	Effingham	Effingham	65.00	80.60	80.60
3410	-	104	-	Effingham	Effingham	270.00	334.80	334.80
3411	-	100	-	Effingham	Effingham	75.00	93.00	93.00
3412	-	30	-	Effingham	Effingham	70.00	86.80	86.80
3413	-	25	-	Effingham	Effingham	30.00	37.20	37.20
3414	-	6	-	Effingham	Effingham	30.00	37.20	37.20
3415	-	30	-	Effingham	Effingham	30.00	37.20	37.20
3416	-	80	-	Effingham	Effingham	180.00	223.20	223.20
3417	-	14	-	Effingham	Effingham	28.00	34.72	34.72
3418	-	60	-	Effingham	Hampton Falls	10.00	12.40	-
3419	-	200	-	Effingham	Effingham	30.00	37.20	49.60
3420	-	100	-	Effingham	Effingham	170.00	210.80	-
3421	-	90	-	Effingham	Effingham	47.00	58.28	-
3422	-	48	-	Effingham	Effingham	24.00	29.76	298.84
3423	-	190	-	Effingham	Effingham	350.00	434.00	434.00
3424	-	50	-	Effingham	Durham	25.00	31.00	31.00
3425	-	40	-	Effingham	Effingham	85.00	105.40	105.40
3426	-	1	-	Effingham	Effingham	100.00	124.00	124.00
3501	-	12	-	Effingham	Effingham	30.00	37.20	-
3502	-	200	-	Effingham	Effingham	250.00	310.00	-
3503	-	50	-	Effingham	Effingham	12.50	15.50	-
3504	-	50	-	Effingham	Effingham	20.50	25.42	-
3505	-	33	-	Effingham	Effingham	25.00	31.00	

1798 DIRECT TAX

Pg/No	Occupant Surname	Occupant First Name	Owner Surname	Owner First Name	Dwg #	Val $	Expt Acr
3506	Unimproved	-	Dearborn	John S.	-	-	-
3507	Unimproved	-	Dearborn	John S.	-	-	-
3508	Drake	Abraham	Drake	Abraham	-	-	-
3509	Unimproved	-	Drake	Abraham	-	-	-
3510	Unimproved	-	Drake	Abraham	-	-	-
3511	Unimproved	-	Drake	Abraham	-	-	-
3512	Unimproved	-	Drake	Abraham	-	-	-
3513	Drake	John	Drake	John	1	30	-
3514	Unimproved	-	Drake	John	-	-	-
3515	Unimproved	-	Drake	John	-	-	-
3516	Unimproved	-	Drake	John	-	-	-
3517	Unimproved	-	Drake	John	-	-	-
3518	Drake	John, Jr.	Drake	John, Jr.	-	-	-
3519	Unimproved	-	Drake	John, Jr.	-	-	-
3520	Unimproved	-	Drake	John, Jr.	-	-	-
3521	Unimproved	-	Drake	Jonathan	-	-	-
3522	Drake	Joseph	Drake	Joseph	1	60	-
3523	Unimproved	-	Drake	Joseph	-	-	-
3524	Unimproved	-	Drake	Joseph	-	-	-
3525	Unimproved	-	Drake	Joseph	-	-	-
3526	Unimproved	-	Drake	Nathaniel	-	-	-
3601	Heirn	John	Emerson	Timothy	1	12	-
3602	Heirn	John	Emerson	Timothy	-	-	-
3603	Unimproved	-	Emerson	Timothy	-	-	-
3604	Unimproved	-	Emerson	Timothy	-	-	-
3605	Unimproved	-	Fisher	John	-	-	-
3606	Unimproved	-	Fisher	John	-	-	-
3607	Glidden	Nicholas	Glidden	Nicholas	1	20	-
3608	Hobbs	Benjamin	Hobbs	Benjamin	-	-	-
3609	Hobbs	Benjamin, Jr.	Hobbs	Benjamin, Jr.	1	20	-
3610	Unimproved	-	Hobbs	Benjamin, Jr.	-	-	-
3611	Unimproved	-	Hobbs	Benjamin, Jr.	-	-	-
3612	Unimproved	-	Hobbs	James	-	-	-
3613	Hobbs	Jonathan	Hobbs	Jonathan	1	25	-
3614	Unimproved	-	Hobbs	Jonathan	-	-	-
3615	Hobbs	Morris	Hobbs	Morris	1	40	-
3616	Hobbs	Nathaniel	Hobbs	Nathaniel	1	50	-
3617	Unimproved	-	Hobbs	Nathaniel	-	-	-
3618	Unimproved	-	Hobbs	Nathaniel	-	-	-
3619	Unimproved	-	Hobbs	Nathaniel	-	-	-
3620	Unimproved	-	Hobbs	Nathaniel	-	-	-
3621	Unimproved	-	Hall	Samuel	-	-	-
3622	Unimproved	-	Jaffrey	George	-	-	-
3623	Unimproved	-	Leavitt	Moses	-	-	-
3624	Unimproved	-	Leavitt	Moses	-	-	-
3625	Unimproved	-	Leavitt	Benjamin	-	-	-
3626	Lamper	Benjamin	Lamper	Benjamin	1	50	-

NEW HAMPSHIRE DISTRICT 13

Pg/No	Ext Per	Acr	Per	Property Location	Residence of Owner	Value $	Eq. Val $	Total $
3506	-	30	-	Effingham	Effingham	40.00	49.60	-
3507	-	10	-	Effingham	Effingham	20.00	24.80	493.52
3508	-	220	-	Effingham	Effingham	1000.00	1240.00	-
3509	-	56	-	Effingham	Effingham	15.00	18.60	-
3510	-	36	-	Effingham	Effingham	12.00	14.88	-
3511	-	100	-	Effingham	Effingham	25.00	31.00	-
3512	-	18	-	Effingham	Effingham	6.00	7.44	1311.92
3513	-	150	-	Effingham	Effingham	540.00	669.60	-
3514	-	200	-	Effingham	Effingham	100.00	124.00	-
3515	-	200	-	Effingham	Effingham	130.00	161.20	-
3516	-	200	-	Effingham	Effingham	130.00	161.20	-
3517	-	56	-	Effingham	Effingham	15.00	18.60	1134.60
3518	-	95	-	Effingham	Effingham	370.00	458.80	-
3519	-	56	-	Effingham	Effingham	20.00	24.80	-
3520	-	28	-	Effingham	Effingham	10.00	12.40	496.00
3521	-	50	-	Effingham	North Hampton	15.00	18.60	18.60
3522	-	200	-	Effingham	Effingham	820.00	1016.80	-
3523	-	56	-	Effingham	Effingham	15.00	18.60	-
3524	-	48	-	Effingham	Effingham	15.00	18.60	-
3525	-	28	-	Effingham	Effingham	10.00	12.40	1066.40
3526	-	200	-	Effingham	North Hampton	100.00	124.00	124.00
3601	-	200	-	Effingham	Durham	237.00	293.88	-
3602	-	200	-	Effingham	Durham	100.00	124.00	-
3603	-	56	-	Effingham	Durham	20.00	24.80	-
3604	-	155	-	Effingham	Durham	100.00	124.00	566.68
3605	-	200	-	Effingham	Portsmouth	50.00	62.00	-
3606	-	56	-	Effingham	Portsmouth	14.00	17.36	79.36
3607	-	39	-	Effingham	Effingham	118.00	146.32	146.32
3608	-	56	-	Effingham	Effingham	214.00	265.36	265.36
3609	-	116	-	Effingham	Effingham	268.00	332.32	-
3610	-	56	-	Effingham	Effingham	15.00	18.60	-
3611	-	56	-	Effingham	Effingham	15.00	18.60	369.52
3612	-	15	-	Effingham	Parsonfield, MA	100.00	124.00	124.00
3613	-	100	-	Effingham	Effingham	300.00	372.00	-
3614	-	50	-	Effingham	Effingham	25.00	31.00	403.00
3615	-	100	-	Effingham	Effingham	350.00	434.00	434.00
3616	-	142	-	Effingham	Effingham	484.00	600.16	-
3617	-	56	-	Effingham	Effingham	15.00	18.60	-
3618	-	56	-	Effingham	Effingham	15.00	18.60	-
3619	-	56	-	Effingham	Effingham	15.00	18.60	-
3620	-	36	-	Effingham	Effingham	12.00	14.88	670.84
3621	-	200	-	Effingham	Wakefield	120.00	148.80	148.80
3622	-	105	-	Effingham	Portsmouth	105.00	130.20	130.20
3623	-	123	-	Effingham	North Hampton	100.00	124.00	-
3624	-	56	-	Effingham	North Hampton	20.00	24.80	148.80
3625	-	168	-	Effingham	North Hampton	90.00	111.60	111.60
3626	-	75	-	Effingham	Effingham	325.00	403.00	403.00

1798 DIRECT TAX

Pg/No	Occupant Surname	Occupant First Name	Owner Surname	Owner First Name	Dwg #	Val $	Expt Acr
3701	Lamper	John	Lamper	John	-	-	-
3702	Leavitt	Carr	Leavitt	Carr	-	-	-
3703	Unimproved	-	Leavitt	Carr	-	-	-
3704	Unimproved	-	Leavitt	Carr	-	-	-
3705	Unimproved	-	Leavitt	Carr	-	-	-
3706	Unimproved	-	Leavitt	Carr	-	-	-
3707	Unimproved	-	Leavitt	Carr	-	-	-
3708	Leavitt	John	Leavitt	John	1	60	-
3709	Unimproved	-	Leavitt	John	-	-	-
3710	Leavitt	Jeremiah	Leavitt	Jeremiah	1	10	-
3711	Leavitt	Morris	Leavitt	Morris	1	20	-
3712	Leavitt	Morris	Leavitt	Morris	-	-	-
3713	Leavitt	Simon	Leavitt	Simon	1	40	-
3714	Unimproved	-	Leavitt	Simon	-	-	-
3715	Littlefield	Henry	Littlefield	Henry	1	15	-
3716	Lord	Isaac	Lord	Isaac	3	35	-
3717	Unimproved	-	Lord	Isaac	-	-	-
3718	Unimproved	-	Lord	Isaac	-	-	-
3719	Lord	Thomas	Lord	Thomas	1	30	-
3720	Unimproved	-	Leavitt	Thomas	-	-	-
3721	Unimproved	-	Marston	Levi	-	-	-
3722	Marston	Abraham	Marston	Abraham	-	-	-
3723	Unimproved	-	Marston	Abraham	-	-	-
3724	Unimproved	-	Marston	Abraham	-	-	-
3725	Unimproved	-	Marston	Abraham	-	-	-
3726	Unimproved	-	Marston	Abraham	-	-	-
3727	Unimproved	-	Marston	Abraham	-	-	-
3801	Marston	Jeremiah	Marston	Jeremiah	1	20	-
3802	Unimproved	-	Marston	Jeremiah	-	-	-
3803	Unimproved	-	Marston	Jeremiah	-	-	-
3804	Unimproved	-	Marston	Jeremiah	-	-	-
3805	Unimproved	-	Marston	Jeremiah	-	-	-
3806	Maloon	Joseph, Jr.	Meloon	Joseph, Jr.	-	-	-
3807	Meloon	Samuel	Meloon	Samuel	-	-	-
3808	Unimproved	-	Meloon	Samuel	-	-	-
3809	Morgan	Parker	Morgan	Parker	1	12	-
3810	Moulton	Jonathan	Moulton	Jonathan	-	-	-
3811	Moulton	Redmond	Moulton	Redmond	-	-	-
3812	Unimproved	-	Moulton	Redmond	-	-	-
3813	Unimproved	-	Moulton	Redmond	-	-	-
3814	Unimproved	-	Moulton	Redmond	-	-	-
3815	Unimproved	-	Morgan	Isaiah	-	-	-
3816	Unimproved	-	Noys	Edmond	-	-	-
3817	Unimproved	-	Noys	Edmond	-	-	-
3818	Palmer	Joseph	Palmer	Joseph	1	7	-
3819	Palmer	Stephen	Palmer	Stephen	1	15	-
3820	Philbrick	Samuel	Philbrick	Samuel	1	30	-

NEW HAMPSHIRE DISTRICT 13

Pg/No	Ext Per	Acr	Per	Property Location	Residence of Owner	Value $	Eq. Val $	Total $
3701	-	75	-	Effingham	Effingham	255.00	316.20	316.20
3702	-	232	-	Effingham	Effingham	841.00	1042.84	-
3703	-	100	-	Effingham	Effingham	150.00	186.00	-
3704	-	80	-	Effingham	Effingham	100.00	124.00	-
3705	-	70	-	Effingham	Effingham	85.00	105.40	-
3706	-	200	-	Effingham	Effingham	150.00	186.00	-
3707	-	28	-	Effingham	Effingham	7.00	8.68	1652.92
3708	-	180	-	Effingham	Effingham	495.00	613.80	-
3709	-	25	-	Effingham	Effingham	12.00	14.88	628.68
3710	-	100	-	Effingham	Effingham	400.00	496.00	496.00
3711	-	78	-	Effingham	Effingham	324.00	401.76	-
3712	-	25	-	Effingham	Effingham	12.00	14.88	416.64
3713	-	56	-	Effingham	Effingham	167.00	207.08	-
3714	-	56	-	Effingham	Effingham	30.00	37.20	244.28
3715	-	36	-	Effingham	Effingham	107.00	132.68	132.68
3716	-	100	-	Effingham	Effingham	405.00	502.20	-
3717	-	100	-	Effingham	Effingham	150.00	186.00	-
3718	-	40	-	Effingham	Effingham	100.00	124.00	812.20
3719	-	180	-	Effingham	Effingham	330.00	409.20	-
3720	-	240	-	Effingham	North Hampton	150.00	186.00	-
3721	-	100	-	Effingham	Effingham	50.00	62.00	657.20
3722	-	200	-	Effingham	Effingham	540.00	669.60	-
3723	-	150	-	Effingham	Effingham	45.00	55.80	-
3724	-	100	-	Effingham	Effingham	50.00	62.00	-
3725	-	50	-	Effingham	Effingham	30.00	37.20	-
3726	-	50	-	Effingham	Effingham	10.00	12.40	-
3727	-	50	-	Effingham	Effingham	15.00	18.60	855.60
3801	-	200	-	Effingham	Effingham	480.00	595.20	-
3802	-	56	-	Effingham	Effingham	15.00	18.60	-
3803	-	100	-	Effingham	Effingham	50.00	62.00	-
3804	-	24	-	Effingham	Effingham	10.00	12.40	-
3805	-	100	-	Effingham	Effingham	80.00	99.20	787.40
3806	-	100	-	Effingham	Effingham	100.00	124.00	124.00
3807	-	140	-	Effingham	Parsonfield, MA	140.00	173.60	-
3808	-	100	-	Effingham	Parsonfield, MA	100.00	124.00	297.60
3809	-	56	-	Effingham	Effingham	52.00	64.48	64.48
3810	-	100	-	Effingham	Effingham	250.00	310.00	310.00
3811	-	210	-	Effingham	Effingham	534.00	662.16	-
3812	-	28	-	Effingham	Effingham	7.00	8.68	-
3813	-	17	-	Effingham	Effingham	7.00	8.68	-
3814	-	95	-	Effingham	Effingham	75.00	93.00	772.52
3815	-	100	-	Effingham	Effingham	100.00	124.00	124.00
3816	-	56	-	Effingham	Seabrook	14.00	17.36	-
3817	-	200	-	Effingham	Seabrook	50.00	62.00	79.36
3818	-	49	-	Effingham	Effingham	27.00	33.48	33.48
3819	-	100	-	Effingham	Effingham	245.00	303.80	303.80
3820	-	67	-	Effingham	Effingham	164.00	203.36	203.36

1798 DIRECT TAX

Pg/No	Occupant Surname	Occupant First Name	Owner Surname	Owner First Name	Dwg #	Val $	Expt Acr
3821	Philbrick	Simon	Philbrick	Simon	-	-	-
3822	Unimproved	-	Philbrick	Simon	-	-	-
3823	Unimproved	-	Pinkham	Thomas	-	-	-
3824	Unimproved	-	Pinkham	Thomas	-	-	-
3825	Unimproved	-	Pinkham	Thomas	-	-	-
3826	Pitman	John	Pitman	John	-	-	-
3901	Unimproved	-	Philbrick	Joseph	-	-	-
3902	Unimproved	-	Page	Coffin	-	-	-
3903	Unimproved	-	Pearson	Thomas	-	-	-
3904	Unimproved	-	Steel	Jonathan	-	-	-
3905	Unimproved	-	Steel	Jonathan	-	-	-
3906	Unimproved	-	Steel	Jonathan	-	-	-
3907	Unimproved	-	Steel	Jonathan	-	-	-
3908	Unimproved	-	Steel	Jonathan	-	-	-
3909	Unimproved	-	Steel	Jonathan	-	-	-
3910	Unimproved	-	Steel	Jonathan	-	-	-
3911	Swasey	Nathaniel	Swasey	Nathaniel	1	25	-
3912	Unimproved	-	Taylor	Abraham	-	-	-
3913	Taylor	John	Taylor	John	1	30	-
3914	Taylor	John, Jr.	Taylor	John, Jr.	1	30	-
3915	Unimproved	-	Taylor	John, Jr.	-	-	-
3916	Unimproved	-	Taylor	John, Jr.	-	-	-
3917	Taylor	Josiah	Taylor	Josiah	1	40	-
3918	Taylor	Richard	Taylor	Richard	1	40	-
3919	Tibbets	Henry	Tibbets	Henry	1	10	-
3920	Titcomb	James	Titcomb	James	-	-	-
3921	Titcomb	Joshua	Titcomb	Joshua	-	-	-
3922	Towle	Amos	Towle	Amos	-	-	-
3923	Towle	Ezra	Towle	Ezra	-	-	-
3924	Towle	Joseph	Towle	Joseph	1	90	-
3925	Unimproved	-	Towle	Joseph	-	-	-
3926	Towle	Joseph, Jr.	Towle	Joseph, Jr.	1	20	-
4001	Towle	Stephen	Towle	Stephen	1	15	-
4002	Towle	William	Towle	William	1	35	-
4003	Unimproved	-	Towle	William	-	-	-
4004	Unimproved	-	Towle	William	-	-	-
4005	Varney	Isaiah	Varney	Isaiah	1	25	-
4006	Ward	Jonathan	Ward	Jonathan	-	-	-
4007	Wedgwood	John	Wedgwood	John	1	12	-
4008	Wedgwood	Josiah	Wedgwood	Josiah	1	60	-
4009	Welch	Roger G.	Welch	Roger G.	-	-	-
4010	Unimproved	-	Young	David	-	-	-
4011	Young	Timothy	Young	Timothy	1	16	-
4012	Unimproved	-	Unknown	-	-	-	-
4013	Unimproved	-	Unknown	-	-	-	-
4014	Unimproved	-	Unknown	-	-	-	-
4015	Unimproved	-	Unknown	-	-	-	-

NEW HAMPSHIRE DISTRICT 13

Pg/No	Ext Per	Acr	Per	Property Location	Residence of Owner	Value $	Eq. Val $	Total $
3821	-	56	-	Effingham	Effingham	277.00	343.48	-
3822	-	49	-	Effingham	Effingham	49.00	60.76	404.24
3823	-	400	-	Effingham	Durham	200.00	248.00	-
3824	-	100	-	Effingham	Durham	50.00	62.00	-
3825	-	100	-	Effingham	Durham	100.00	124.00	434.00
3826	-	50	-	Effingham	Effingham	50.00	62.00	62.00
3901	-	56	-	Effingham	Hampton	40.00	49.60	49.60
3902	-	56	-	Effingham	North Hampton	20.00	24.80	24.80
3903	-	200	-	Effingham	Parsonfield, MA	150.00	186.00	186.00
3904	-	100	-	Effingham	Durham	50.00	62.00	-
3905	-	60	-	Effingham	Durham	60.00	74.40	-
3906	-	100	-	Effingham	Durham	50.00	62.00	-
3907	-	90	-	Effingham	Durham	90.00	111.60	-
3908	-	100	-	Effingham	Durham	25.00	31.00	-
3909	-	100	-	Effingham	Durham	25.00	31.00	-
3910	-	25	-	Effingham	Durham	12.00	14.88	386.88
3911	-	50	-	Effingham	Effingham	125.00	155.00	155.00
3912	-	100	-	Effingham	North Hampton	30.00	37.20	37.20
3913	-	16	-	Effingham	Effingham	93.00	115.32	115.32
3914	-	256	-	Effingham	Effingham	728.00	902.72	-
3915	-	80	-	Effingham	Effingham	100.00	124.00	-
3916	-	100	-	Effingham	Effingham	75.00	93.00	1119.72
3917	-	32	-	Effingham	Effingham	82.00	101.68	101.68
3918	-	100	-	Effingham	Effingham	260.00	322.40	322.40
3919	-	86	-	Effingham	Effingham	90.00	111.60	111.60
3920	-	200	-	Effingham	Effingham	755.00	936.20	936.20
3921	-	56	-	Effingham	Effingham	224.00	277.76	277.76
3922	-	200	-	Effingham	Effingham	150.00	186.00	186.00
3923	-	120	-	Effingham	Effingham	100.00	124.00	124.00
3924	-	200	-	Effingham	Effingham	530.00	657.20	-
3925	-	50	-	Effingham	Effingham	80.00	99.20	756.40
3926	-	90	-	Effingham	Effingham	300.00	372.00	372.00
4001	-	90	-	Effingham	Effingham	320.00	396.80	396.80
4002	-	76	-	Effingham	Effingham	297.00	368.28	-
4003	-	200	-	Effingham	Effingham	200.00	248.00	-
4004	-	200	-	Effingham	Effingham	200.00	248.00	864.28
4005	-	-	40	Effingham	Effingham	30.00	37.20	37.20
4006	-	50	-	Effingham	Effingham	75.00	93.00	93.00
4007	-	100	-	Effingham	Effingham	227.00	281.48	281.48
4008	-	70	-	Effingham	Effingham	280.00	347.20	347.20
4009	-	150	-	Effingham	Effingham	100.00	124.00	124.00
4010	-	100	-	Effingham	Gilmanton	100.00	124.00	124.00
4011	-	64	-	Effingham	Effingham	165.00	204.60	204.60
4012	-	38	-	Effingham	Effingham	16.00	19.84	19.84
4013	-	200	-	Effingham	Effingham	50.00	62.00	62.00
4014	-	100	-	Effingham	Effingham	50.00	62.00	62.00
4015	-	56	-	Effingham	Effingham	10.00	12.40	12.40

1798 DIRECT TAX

Pg/No	Occupant Surname	Occupant First Name	Owner Surname	Owner First Name	Dwg #	Val $	Expt Acr
4016	Unimproved	-	Unknown	-	-	-	-
4017	Unimproved	-	Unknown	-	-	-	-
4018	Unimproved	-	Unknown	-	-	-	-
4019	Unimproved	-	Unknown	-	-	-	-
4020	Unimproved	-	Unknown	-	-	-	-
4021	Unimproved	-	Unknown	-	-	-	-
4022	Unimproved	-	Unknown	-	-	-	-
4023	Unimproved	-	Unknown	-	-	-	-
4024	Unimproved	-	Unknown	-	-	-	-
4025	Unimproved	-	Unknown	-	-	-	-
4026	Unimproved	-	Unknown	-	-	-	-
4101	Unimproved	-	Unknown	-	-	-	-
4102	Unimproved	-	Unknown	-	-	-	-
4103	Unimproved	-	Unknown	-	-	-	-
4104	Unimproved	-	Unknown	-	-	-	-
4105	Unimproved	-	Unknown	-	-	-	-
4106	Unimproved	-	Unknown	-	-	-	-
4107	Unimproved	-	Unknown	-	-	-	-
4108	Unimproved	-	Unknown	-	-	-	-
4109	Unimproved	-	Unknown	-	-	-	-
4110	Unimproved	-	Unknown	-	-	-	-
4111	Unimproved	-	Unknown	-	-	-	-
4112	Unimproved	-	Unknown	-	-	-	-
4113	Unimproved	-	Unknown	-	-	-	-
4114	Unimproved	-	Unknown	-	-	-	-
4115	Unimproved	-	Unknown	-	-	-	-
4116	Unimproved	-	Unknown	-	-	-	-
4117	Unimproved	-	Unknown	-	-	-	-
4118	Unimproved	-	Unknown	-	-	-	-
4119	Unimproved	-	Unknown	-	-	-	-
4120	Unimproved	-	Unknown	-	-	-	-
4121	Unimproved	-	Unknown	-	-	-	-
4122	Unimproved	-	Unknown	-	-	-	-
4123	Unimproved	-	Unknown	-	-	-	-
4124	Unimproved	-	Unknown	-	-	-	-
4125	Unimproved	-	Unknown	-	-	-	-
4126	Unimproved	-	Unknown	-	-	-	-
4201	Unimproved	-	Unknown	-	-	-	-
4202	Unimproved	-	Unknown	-	-	-	-
4203	Unimproved	-	Unknown	-	-	-	-
4204	Unimproved	-	Unknown	-	-	-	-
4205	Unimproved	-	Unknown	-	-	-	-
4206	Unimproved	-	Unknown	-	-	-	-
4207	Unimproved	-	Unknown	-	-	-	-
4208	Unimproved	-	Unknown	-	-	-	-
4209	Unimproved	-	Unknown	-	-	-	-
4210	Unimproved	-	Unknown	-	-	-	-

NEW HAMPSHIRE DISTRICT 13

Pg/No	Ext Per	Acr	Per	Property Location	Residence of Owner	Value $	Eq. Val $	Total $
4016	-	200	-	Effingham	Effingham	100.00	124.00	124.00
4017	-	200	-	Effingham	Effingham	50.00	62.00	62.00
4018	-	100	-	Effingham	Effingham	50.00	62.00	62.00
4019	-	56	-	Effingham	Effingham	20.00	24.80	24.80
4020	-	200	-	Effingham	Effingham	50.00	62.00	62.00
4021	-	56	-	Effingham	Effingham	10.00	12.40	12.40
4022	-	200	-	Effingham	Effingham	24.00	29.76	29.76
4023	-	200	-	Effingham	Effingham	40.00	49.60	49.60
4024	-	56	-	Effingham	Effingham	6.00	7.44	7.44
4025	-	100	-	Effingham	Effingham	50.00	62.00	62.00
4026	-	56	-	Effingham	Effingham	40.00	49.60	49.60
4101	-	56	-	Effingham	Effingham	15.00	18.60	18.60
4102	-	100	-	Effingham	Effingham	40.00	49.60	49.60
4103	-	200	-	Effingham	Effingham	100.00	124.00	124.00
4104	-	100	-	Effingham	Effingham	25.00	31.00	31.00
4105	-	56	-	Effingham	Effingham	10.00	12.40	12.40
4106	-	200	-	Effingham	Effingham	100.00	124.00	124.00
4107	-	56	-	Effingham	Effingham	50.00	62.00	62.00
4108	-	200	-	Effingham	Effingham	50.00	62.00	62.00
4109	-	200	-	Effingham	Effingham	50.00	62.00	62.00
4110	-	56	-	Effingham	Effingham	15.00	18.60	18.60
4111	-	40	-	Effingham	Effingham	35.00	43.40	43.40
4112	-	56	-	Effingham	Effingham	16.00	19.84	19.84
4113	-	56	-	Effingham	Effingham	20.00	24.80	24.80
4114	-	200	-	Effingham	Effingham	30.00	37.20	37.20
4115	-	56	-	Effingham	Effingham	18.00	22.32	22.32
4116	-	100	-	Effingham	Effingham	40.00	49.60	49.60
4117	-	56	-	Effingham	Effingham	15.00	18.60	18.60
4118	-	39	-	Effingham	Effingham	7.00	8.68	8.68
4119	-	200	-	Effingham	Effingham	50.00	62.00	62.00
4120	-	56	-	Effingham	Effingham	15.00	18.60	18.60
4121	-	100	-	Effingham	Effingham	100.00	124.00	124.00
4122	-	28	-	Effingham	Effingham	8.00	9.92	9.92
4123	-	56	-	Effingham	Effingham	10.00	12.40	12.40
4124	-	56	-	Effingham	Effingham	15.00	18.60	18.60
4125	-	200	-	Effingham	Effingham	100.00	124.00	124.00
4126	-	200	-	Effingham	Effingham	200.00	248.00	248.00
4201	-	56	-	Effingham	Effingham	16.00	19.84	19.84
4202	-	150	-	Effingham	Effingham	100.00	124.00	124.00
4203	-	56	-	Effingham	Effingham	10.00	12.40	12.40
4204	-	200	-	Effingham	Effingham	50.00	62.00	62.00
4205	-	200	-	Effingham	Effingham	60.00	74.40	74.40
4206	-	56	-	Effingham	Effingham	10.00	12.40	12.40
4207	-	200	-	Effingham	Effingham	120.00	148.80	148.80
4208	-	200	-	Effingham	Effingham	100.00	124.00	124.00
4209	-	145	-	Effingham	Effingham	20.00	24.80	24.80
4210	-	100	-	Effingham	Effingham	100.00	124.00	124.00

1798 DIRECT TAX

Pg/No	Occupant Surname	Occupant First Name	Owner Surname	Owner First Name	Dwg #	Val $	Expt Acr
4211	Unimproved	-	Unknown	-	-	-	-
4212	Unimproved	-	Unknown	-	-	-	-
4213	Unimproved	-	Unknown	-	-	-	-
4214	Unimproved	-	Unknown	-	-	-	-
4215	Unimproved	-	Unknown	-	-	-	-
4216	Unimproved	-	Unknown	-	-	-	-
4217	Unimproved	-	Unknown	-	-	-	-
4218	Unimproved	-	Unknown	-	-	-	-
4219	Unimproved	-	Unknown	-	-	-	-
4220	Unimproved	-	Unknown	-	-	-	-
4221	Unimproved	-	Unknown	-	-	-	-
4222	Unimproved	-	Unknown	-	-	-	-
4223	Unimproved	-	Unknown	-	-	-	-
4224	Unimproved	-	Unknown	-	-	-	-
4225	Unimproved	-	Unknown	-	-	-	-
4226	Unimproved	-	Unknown	-	-	-	-
4301	Unimproved	-	Unknown	-	-	-	-
4302	Unimproved	-	Unknown	-	-	-	-
4303	Unimproved	-	Unknown	-	-	-	-
4304	Unimproved	-	Unknown	-	-	-	-
4305	Unimproved	-	Unknown	-	-	-	-
4306	Unimproved	-	Unknown	-	-	-	-
4307	Unimproved	-	Unknown	-	-	-	-
4308	Unimproved	-	Unknown	-	-	-	-
4309	Allard	Jonathan, Jr.	Allard	Jonathan, Jr.	1	90	-
4310	Allard	Shadrach	Allard	Shadrach	-	-	-
4311	Barker	John	Barker	John	1	30	-
4312	Bennett	Abraham	Bennett	Abraham	1	20	-
4313	Unimproved	-	Bennett	Abraham	-	-	-
4314	Unimproved	-	Bennett	Abraham	-	-	-
4315	Bennett	John, Jr.	Bennett	John, Jr.	-	-	-
4316	Bennett	John, Jr.	Bennett	John, Jr.	1	5	-
4317	Unimproved	-	Bennett	John, Jr.	-	-	-
4318	Unimproved	-	Bennett	John, Jr.	-	-	-
4319	Berry	Benjamin	Berry	Benjamin	-	-	-
4320	-	-	Berry	Benjamin	-	-	-
4321	Berry	John	Berry	John	1	50	-
4322	-	-	Berry	John	-	-	-
4323	Berry	Joseph	Berry	Joseph	-	-	-
4324	-	-	Berry	Joseph	-	-	-
4325	-	-	Berry	Joseph	-	-	-
4326	Bickford	Abraham	Bickford	Abraham	-	-	-
4401	Berry	Stephen, Jr.	Berry	Stephen, Jr.	1	15	-
4402	Unimproved	-	Berry	Stephen, Jr.	-	-	-
4403	Unimproved	-	Berry	Stephen, Jr.	-	-	-
4404	Unimproved	-	Blydenburgh	John	-	-	-
4405	Unimproved	-	Blydenburgh	John	-	-	-

NEW HAMPSHIRE DISTRICT 13

Pg/No	Ext Per	Acr	Per	Property Location	Residence of Owner	Value $	Eq. Val $	Total $
4211	-	56	-	Effingham	Effingham	10.00	12.40	12.40
4212	-	56	-	Effingham	Effingham	24.00	29.76	29.76
4213	-	56	-	Effingham	Effingham	8.00	9.92	9.92
4214	-	200	-	Effingham	Effingham	24.00	29.76	29.76
4215	-	56	-	Effingham	Effingham	14.00	17.36	17.36
4216	-	200	-	Effingham	Effingham	60.00	74.40	74.40
4217	-	28	-	Effingham	Effingham	8.00	9.92	9.92
4218	-	200	-	Effingham	Effingham	80.00	99.20	99.20
4219	-	56	-	Effingham	Effingham	10.00	12.40	12.40
4220	-	200	-	Effingham	Effingham	50.00	62.00	62.00
4221	-	56	-	Effingham	Effingham	8.00	9.92	9.92
4222	-	200	-	Effingham	Effingham	40.00	49.60	49.60
4223	-	56	-	Effingham	Effingham	8.00	9.92	9.92
4224	-	200	-	Effingham	Effingham	200.00	248.00	248.00
4225	-	50	-	Effingham	Effingham	6.00	7.44	7.44
4226	-	56	-	Effingham	Effingham	10.00	12.40	12.40
4301	-	120	-	Effingham	Effingham	20.00	24.80	-
4302	-	56	-	Effingham	Effingham	10.00	12.40	-
4303	-	56	-	Effingham	Effingham	10.00	12.40	-
4304	-	200	-	Effingham	Effingham	100.00	124.00	-
4305	-	56	-	Effingham	Effingham	30.00	37.20	-
4306	-	56	-	Effingham	Effingham	8.00	9.92	-
4307	-	56	-	Effingham	Effingham	10.00	12.40	-
4308	-	56	-	Effingham	Effingham	10.00	12.40	-
4309	-	125	-	New Durham	New Durham	495.00	613.80	613.80
4310	-	100	-	New Durham	New Durham	200.00	248.00	248.00
4311	-	-	-	New Durham	New Durham	30.00	37.20	37.20
4312	-	75	-	New Durham	New Durham	275.00	341.00	-
4313	-	100	-	New Durham	New Durham	50.00	62.00	-
4314	-	100	-	New Durham	New Durham	100.00	124.00	527.00
4315	-	99	-	New Durham	New Durham	780.00	967.20	-
4316	-	55	-	New Durham	New Durham	410.00	508.40	-
4317	-	80	-	New Durham	New Durham	40.00	49.60	-
4318	-	20	-	New Durham	New Durham	10.00	12.40	1537.60
4319	-	199	-	New Durham	New Durham	418.00	518.32	-
4320	-	125	-	New Durham	New Durham	125.00	155.00	673.32
4321	-	87	-	New Durham	New Durham	400.00	496.00	-
4322	-	50	-	New Durham	New Durham	270.00	344.72	840.72
4323	-	86	80	New Durham	New Durham	374.00	463.76	-
4324	-	100	-	New Durham	New Durham	300.00	372.00	-
4325	-	125	-	New Durham	New Durham	50.00	62.00	897.76
4326	-	99	-	New Durham	New Durham	729.00	903.96	903.96
4401	-	50	-	New Durham	New Durham	265.00	328.60	-
4402	-	40	-	New Durham	New Durham	25.00	31.00	-
4403	-	12	80	New Durham	New Durham	30.50	37.82	397.42
4404	-	50	-	New Durham	Durham	50.00	62.00	-
4405	-	125	-	New Durham	Durham	250.00	310.00	372.00

1798 DIRECT TAX

Pg/No	Occupant Surname	Occupant First Name	Owner Surname	Owner First Name	Dwg #	Val $	Expt Acr
4406	Bickford	Andrew	Bickford	Andrew	1	20	-
4407	Bickford	John	Bickford	John	-	-	-
4408	Bickford	Jonathan	Bickford	Jonathan	1	2	-
4409	Bickford	Joseph	Bickford	Joseph	1	1	-
4410	Bickford	Samuel	Bickford	Samuel	1	1	-
4411	Bickford	Samuel	Bickford	Samuel	-	-	-
4412	Boody	Zachariah	Boody	Zachariah	-	-	-
4413	-	-	Boody	Zachariah	-	-	-
4414	Unimproved	-	Bowles	Samuel	-	-	-
4415	Bunker	James	Bunker	James	1	2	-
4416	-	-	Burnham	Robert	-	-	-
4417	Burnham	Robert	Burnham	Robert	1	10	-
4418	Unimproved	-	Burnham	Robert	-	-	-
4419	Canney	John	Canney	John	-	-	-
4420	Canney	Thomas	Canney	Thomas	1	30	-
4421	Caverly	Benjamin	Caverly	Benjamin	1	10	-
4422	Caverly	Thomas	Caverly	Thomas	1	2	-
4423	Bickford	John	Canney	Moses	1	10	-
4424	Chamberlain	Abraham	Chamberlain	Abraham	-	-	-
4425	Chamberlain	Ephraim	Chamberlain	Ephraim	-	-	-
4426	Chamberlain	Isaac	Chamberlain	Isaac	1	37	-
4501	Chamberlain	Pensel	Chamberlain	Pensel	1	10	-
4502	Unimproved	-	Chesly	Benjamin	-	-	-
4503	Unimproved	-	Chesly	Joseph	-	-	-
4504	Chesly	Miles	Chesly	Miles	1	4	-
4505	Chesly	Miles	Chesly	Miles	-	-	-
4506	Unimproved	-	Chesly	Samuel	-	-	-
4507	Clark	Haniel	Clark	Haniel	-	-	-
4508	Colomy	Daniel	Colomy	Daniel	-	-	-
4509	-	-	Colomy	Daniel	-	-	-
4510	Colomy	David	Colomy	David	-	-	-
4511	Colomy	John	Colomy	John	-	-	-
4512	Colomy	John	Colomy	John	-	-	-
4513	Colomy	John	Colomy	John	-	-	-
4514	Colomy	John, Jr.	Colomy	John, Jr.	-	-	-
4515	Colomy	Richard	Colomy	Richard	1	20	-
4516	-	-	Clark	Samuel	-	-	-
4517	Davis	Elisha	Davis	Elisha	-	-	-
4518	Unimproved	-	Davis	Elisha	-	-	-
4519	Unimproved	-	Davis	Elisha	-	-	-
4520	Unimproved	-	Davis	Elisha	-	-	-
4521	Unimproved	-	Davis	Elisha	-	-	-
4522	Unimproved	-	Davis	Elisha	-	-	-
4523	Unimproved	-	Davis	Elisha	-	-	-
4524	Unimproved	-	Davis	Elisha	-	-	-
4525	Unimproved	-	Davis	Elisha	-	-	-
4526	Davis	John	Davis	John	-	-	-

NEW HAMPSHIRE DISTRICT 13

Pg/No	Ext Per	Acr	Per	Property Location	Residence of Owner	Value $	Eq. Val $	Total $
4406	-	100	-	New Durham	New Durham	100.00	124.00	124.00
4407	-	89	-	New Durham	New Durham	312.00	386.88	386.88
4408	-	39	-	New Durham	New Durham	116.50	144.46	144.46
4409	-	20	-	New Durham	New Durham	31.00	38.44	38.44
4410	-	125	-	New Durham	New Durham	300.00	372.00	-
4411	-	84	-	New Durham	New Durham	240.00	297.60	669.60
4412	-	90	-	New Durham	New Durham	480.00	595.20	-
4413	-	25	-	New Durham	New Durham	120.00	148.80	744.00
4414	-	70	-	New Durham	Portsmouth	210.00	260.40	260.40
4415	-	35	-	New Durham	New Durham	100.00	124.00	124.00
4416	-	96	-	New Durham	Durham	48.00	59.52	59.52
4417	-	125	-	New Durham	New Durham	150.00	186.00	-
4418	-	62	-	New Durham	New Durham	15.50	19.22	205.22
4419	-	99	-	New Durham	New Durham	700.00	868.00	868.00
4420	-	91	-	New Durham	New Durham	439.00	544.36	544.36
4421	-	62	-	New Durham	New Durham	155.00	192.20	192.20
4422	-	62	-	New Durham	New Durham	147.00	182.28	182.28
4423	-	50	-	New Durham	Madbury	230.00	285.20	285.20
4424	-	99	-	New Durham	New Durham	441.00	546.84	546.84
4425	-	50	-	New Durham	Alton	300.00	372.00	372.00
4426	-	70	-	New Durham	New Durham	354.00	438.96	438.96
4501	-	100	-	New Durham	New Durham	270.00	334.80	334.80
4502	-	100	-	New Durham	Durham	200.00	248.00	248.00
4503	-	125	-	New Durham	Durham	312.50	387.50	387.50
4504	-	125	-	New Durham	New Durham	500.00	620.00	-
4505	-	125	-	New Durham	New Durham	504.00	624.96	1244.96
4506	-	130	-	New Durham	Durham	500.00	620.00	620.00
4507	-	12	80	New Durham	New Durham	110.00	136.40	136.40
4508	-	108	-	New Durham	New Durham	560.00	694.40	-
4509	-	40	-	New Durham	New Durham	120.00	148.80	843.20
4510	-	125	-	New Durham	New Durham	125.00	155.00	155.00
4511	-	176	-	New Durham	New Durham	804.00	996.96	-
4512	-	25	-	New Durham	New Durham	50.00	62.00	-
4513	-	55	-	New Durham	New Durham	55.00	68.20	1127.16
4514	-	125	-	New Durham	New Durham	187.00	231.88	231.88
4515	-	60	-	New Durham	New Durham	210.00	260.40	260.40
4516	-	125	-	New Durham	Middleton	187.00	231.88	231.88
4517	-	199	-	New Durham	New Durham	880.00	1091.20	-
4518	-	100	-	New Durham	New Durham	250.00	310.00	-
4519	-	100	-	New Durham	New Durham	180.00	223.20	-
4520	-	100	-	New Durham	New Durham	120.00	148.80	-
4521	-	7	-	New Durham	New Durham	28.00	34.72	-
4522	-	125	-	New Durham	New Durham	50.00	62.00	-
4523	-	85	-	New Durham	New Durham	43.00	53.32	-
4524	-	26	-	New Durham	New Durham	13.00	16.12	-
4525	-	38	-	New Durham	New Durham	10.00	12.40	1951.76
4526	-	104	-	New Durham	New Durham	250.00	310.00	310.00

1798 DIRECT TAX

Pg/No	Occupant Surname	Occupant First Name	Owner Surname	Owner First Name	Dwg #	Val $	Expt Acr
4601	Davis	George	Davis	George	-	-	-
4602	Davis	George	Davis	George	-	-	-
4603	Davis	George	Davis	George	-	-	-
4604	Davis	George	Davis	George	-	-	-
4605	Davis	Lemuel	Davis	Lemuel	1	20	-
4606	Unimproved	-	Davis	Lemuel	-	-	-
4607	Unimproved	-	Davis	Lemuel	-	-	-
4608	Davis	Solomon	Davis	Solomon	-	-	-
4609	Davis	Winthrop	Davis	Winthrop	-	-	-
4610	Unimproved	-	Davis	Winthrop	-	-	-
4611	Unimproved	-	Davis	Eleazer	-	-	-
4612	Davis	Ebenezer	Davis	Zebulon	-	-	-
4613	Unimproved	-	Davis	Zebulon	-	-	-
4614	Dearing	James	Deering	James	1	10	-
4615	Doe	James	Doe	James	1	1	-
4616	Doe	John	Doe	John	1	12	-
4617	Doe	Josiah	Doe	Josiah	-	-	-
4618	Drew	Solomon	Drew	Solomon	-	-	-
4619	-	-	Davis	Gideon	-	-	-
4620	-	-	Drown	Samuel	-	-	-
4621	-	-	Drown	Samuel	-	-	-
4622	-	-	Drown	Samuel	-	-	-
4623	Unimproved	-	Drew	Elijah	-	-	-
4624	Murray	John	Durgan	Zebulon	1	30	-
4625	Ducoin	Andrew	Ducoin	Andrew	1	10	-
4626	Unimproved	-	Ducoin	Andrew	-	-	-
4701	Durgan	Daniel	Durgan	Daniel	-	-	-
4702	Unimproved	-	Durgan	Daniel	-	-	-
4703	Durgan	George	Durgan	George	-	-	-
4704	Durgan	Lydia	Durgan	Lydia	-	-	-
4705	Unimproved	-	Durgan	Lydia	-	-	-
4706	Edgerly	Caleb	Edgerly	Caleb	-	-	-
4707	Unimproved	-	Edgerly	Caleb	-	-	-
4708	Edgerly	John	Edgerly	John	1	90	-
4709	Edgerly	Joseph	Edgerly	Joseph	-	-	-
4710	Edgerly	Josiah	Edgerly	Josiah	-	-	-
4711	Elkins	David	Elkins	David	-	-	-
4712	Elkins	David	Elkins	David	-	-	-
4713	Elkins	David	Elkins	David	-	-	-
4714	Elkins	David	Elkins	David	-	-	-
4715	Elkins	David	Elkins	David	-	-	-
4716	Elkins	Samuel	Elkins	Samuel	-	-	-
4717	Unimproved	-	Elkins	Samuel	-	-	-
4718	Ellis	David	Ellis	David	-	-	-
4719	Evans	Daniel	Evans	Daniel	1	10	-
4720	Evans	Joseph	Evans	Joseph	1	40	-
4721	Evans	Joseph	Evans	Joseph	-	-	-

NEW HAMPSHIRE DISTRICT 13

Pg/No	Ext Per	Acr	Per	Property Location	Residence of Owner	Value $	Eq. Val $	Total $
4601	-	124	-	New Durham	New Durham	518.00	642.32	-
4602	-	40	-	New Durham	New Durham	40.00	49.60	-
4603	-	24	-	New Durham	New Durham	24.00	29.76	-
4604	-	40	-	New Durham	New Durham	40.00	49.60	771.28
4605	-	125	-	New Durham	New Durham	150.00	186.00	-
4606	-	125	-	New Durham	New Durham	125.00	155.00	-
4607	-	81	-	New Durham	New Durham	20.50	25.42	366.42
4608	-	249	-	New Durham	New Durham	1200.00	1488.00	1488.00
4609	-	99	-	New Durham	New Durham	436.00	540.64	-
4610	-	125	-	New Durham	New Durham	62.00	76.88	617.52
4611	-	125	-	New Durham	Alton	125.00	155.00	155.00
4612	-	97	-	New Durham	Alton	568.00	704.32	-
4613	-	130	-	New Durham	Alton	187.00	231.88	936.20
4614	-	125	-	New Durham	New Durham	275.00	341.00	341.00
4615	-	62	-	New Durham	New Durham	125.00	155.00	155.00
4616	-	54	-	New Durham	New Durham	120.00	148.80	148.80
4617	-	50	-	New Durham	New Durham	100.00	124.00	124.00
4618	-	87	-	New Durham	New Durham	373.00	462.52	462.52
4619	-	100	-	New Durham	Alton	250.00	310.00	310.00
4620	-	100	-	New Durham	Portsmouth	200.00	248.00	-
4621	-	125	-	New Durham	Portsmouth	125.00	155.00	-
4622	-	125	-	New Durham	Portsmouth	125.00	155.00	558.00
4623	-	100	-	New Durham	Northfield, MA	150.00	186.00	186.00
4624	-	114	-	New Durham	Durham	502.00	622.48	622.48
4625	-	50	-	New Durham	New Durham	110.00	136.40	-
4626	-	15	-	New Durham	New Durham	15.00	18.60	155.00
4701	-	24	-	New Durham	New Durham	102.00	126.48	-
4702	-	50	-	New Durham	New Durham	50.00	62.00	188.48
4703	-	100	-	New Durham	New Durham	340.00	421.60	421.60
4704	-	151	-	New Durham	New Durham	794.00	984.56	-
4705	-	62	80	New Durham	New Durham	31.00	38.44	1023.00
4706	-	99	-	New Durham	New Durham	344.00	426.56	-
4707	-	125	-	New Durham	New Durham	125.00	155.00	581.56
4708	-	20	-	New Durham	New Durham	160.00	198.40	198.40
4709	-	62	80	New Durham	New Durham	125.00	155.00	155.00
4710	-	24	-	New Durham	New Durham	120.00	148.80	148.80
4711	-	99	-	New Durham	New Durham	764.00	947.36	-
4712	-	100	-	New Durham	New Durham	150.00	186.00	-
4713	-	45	-	New Durham	New Durham	95.00	117.80	-
4714	-	125	-	New Durham	New Durham	100.00	124.00	-
4715	-	125	-	New Durham	New Durham	31.00	38.44	1413.60
4716	-	125	-	New Durham	New Durham	250.00	310.00	-
4717	-	62	-	New Durham	New Durham	15.50	19.22	329.22
4718	-	100	-	New Durham	New Durham	520.00	644.80	644.80
4719	-	3	-	New Durham	New Durham	55.00	68.20	68.20
4720	-	50	-	New Durham	New Durham	275.00	341.00	-
4721	-	15	80	New Durham	New Durham	108.00	133.92	474.92

1798 DIRECT TAX

Pg/No	Occupant Surname	Occupant First Name	Owner Surname	Owner First Name	Dwg #	Val $	Expt Acr
4722	Folsom	Jonathan	Folsom	Jonathan	-	-	-
4723	French	Thomas	French	Thomas	-	-	-
4724	Unimproved	-	Goodal	Samuel	-	-	-
4725	-	-	Gilman	Joseph	-	-	-
4726	Unimproved	-	Hiner	John H.	-	-	-
4727		-	Hiner	John H.	-	-	-
4801	Kenny	Ichabod	Hanson	Micaiah	1	10	-
4802	Unimproved	-	Hanson	Daniel	-	-	-
4803	Unimproved	-	Hayes	Elihu	-	-	-
4804	Hamons	Samuel	Hayes	Reuben	1	50	-
4805	Cogswell	Joseph	Jaffrey	George	-	-	-
4806	Unimproved	-	Jaffrey	George	-	-	-
4807	Durgan&Wentworth	Jos&Paul	Jewett	James	2	80	-
4808	Jackson	Joseph	Jackson	Joseph	-	-	-
4809	-	-	Jackson	Joseph	-	-	-
4810	Johnson	Nathaniel	Johnson	Nathaniel	1	1	-
4811	Joy	Samuel	Joy	Samuel	-	-	-
4812	Unimproved	-	Joy	Samuel	-	-	-
4813	Jenkins	Ebenezer	Jenkins	Ebenezer	1	30	-
4814	Jennings	Richard	Jennings	Richard	-	-	-
4815	Kelly	David	Kelly	David	1	10	-
4816	Kennison	Joseph	Kennison	Joseph	1	10	-
4817	-	-	Kent	William	-	-	-
4818	Kennison	Nathan	Kennison	Nathan	-	-	-
4819	Unimproved	-	Kennison	Nathan	-	-	-
4820	Unimproved	-	Kennison	Nathan, Jr.	-	-	-
4821	Kennison	Eliaphalet	Kennison	Eliaphalet	1	2	-
4822	-	-	Kent	Richard	-	-	-
4823	Unimproved	-	Knight	Hatevil	-	-	-
4824	Libby	Benjamin	Libby	Benjamin	1	10	-
4825	Edgerly	Thomas	Libby	Abraham	1	10	-
4826	Edgerly	Thomas	Libby	Abraham	-	-	-
4901	Beck	Joseph	Lord	Nathaniel	1	20	-
4902	Leighton	Jacob	Leighton	Jacob	-	-	-
4903	Mason	John	Mason	John	1	90	-
4904	-	-	Mathes	Volentine	-	-	-
4905	Meserve	Joseph	Meserve	Joseph	1	20	-
4906	Mitchel	John	Mitchel	John	-	-	-
4907	Drew	Jonathan	Mooney	Jeremiah	1	10	-
4908	Mooney	Joseph	Mooney	Joseph	-	-	-
4909	-	-	Mooney	Joseph	-	-	-
4910	-	-	Mooney	Stephen	1	75	-
4911	Murray	John	Murray	John	-	-	-
4912	Norton	Thomas	Norton	Thomas	1	75	-
4913	Palmer	Jeremiah	Palmer	Jeremiah	1	65	-
4914	Perkins	Ezekiel	Perkins	Ezekiel	1	10	-
4915	-	-	Pearl	John	-	-	-

NEW HAMPSHIRE DISTRICT 13

Pg/No	Ext Per	Acr	Per	Property Location	Residence of Owner	Value $	Eq. Val $	Total $
4722	-	199	-	New Durham	New Durham	996.00	1235.04	1235.04
4723	-	59	-	New Durham	New Durham	428.00	530.72	530.72
4724	-	62	80	New Durham	New Durham	62.50	77.50	77.50
4725	-	63	-	New Durham	Vermont	126.00	156.24	156.24
4726	-	125	-	New Durham	Middleton	62.50	77.50	-
4727	-	125	-	New Durham	Middleton	187.50	232.50	310.00
4801	-	96	-	New Durham	Alton	313.00	388.12	388.12
4802	-	60	-	New Durham	Durham	60.00	74.40	74.40
4803	-	126	80	New Durham	Madbury	506.00	627.44	627.44
4804	-	100	-	New Durham	Madbury	400.00	496.00	496.00
4805	-	100	-	New Durham	Portsmouth	330.00	409.20	-
4806	-	125	-	New Durham	Portsmouth	375.00	465.00	874.20
4807	-	125	-	New Durham	Dover	385.00	477.40	477.40
4808	-	100	-	New Durham	New Durham	60.00	74.40	-
4809	-	42	-	New Durham	New Durham	30.00	37.20	111.60
4810	-	50	-	New Durham	New Durham	121.00	150.04	151.04
4811	-	112	-	New Durham	New Durham	560.00	694.40	-
4812	-	40	-	New Durham	New Durham	40.00	49.60	744.00
4813	-	100	-	New Durham	New Durham	665.00	824.60	824.60
4814	-	100	-	New Durham	New Durham	100.00	124.00	124.00
4815	-	75	-	New Durham	New Durham	310.00	384.40	384.40
4816	-	100	-	New Durham	New Durham	250.00	310.00	310.00
4817	-	62	80	New Durham	Brookfield	245.00	303.80	303.80
4818	-	99	-	New Durham	New Durham	318.00	394.32	-
4819	-	125	-	New Durham	New Durham	31.50	39.06	433.38
4820	-	125	-	New Durham	New Durham	162.50	201.50	201.50
4821	-	112	-	New Durham	New Durham	140.00	173.60	173.60
4822	-	65	-	New Durham	Durham	125.00	155.00	155.00
4823	-	125	-	New Durham	Rochester	125.00	155.00	155.00
4824	-	50	-	New Durham	New Durham	310.00	384.40	384.40
4825	-	30	-	New Durham	Alton	240.00	297.60	-
4826	-	49	-	New Durham	Alton	24.50	30.38	327.98
4901	-	100	-	New Durham	New Markett	500.00	620.00	620.00
4902	-	124	-	New Durham	New Durham	400.00	496.00	496.00
4903	-	100	-	New Durham	New Durham	300.00	372.00	372.00
4904	-	100	-	New Durham	Durham	120.00	148.80	148.80
4905	-	125	-	New Durham	New Durham	330.00	409.20	409.20
4906	-	62	-	New Durham	New Durham	62.50	77.50	77.50
4907	-	115	-	New Durham	Durham	298.00	369.52	369.52
4908	-	101	80	New Durham	New Durham	283.00	350.92	-
4909	-	50	-	New Durham	New Durham	170.00	210.80	561.72
4910	-	-	-	New Durham	New Durham	75.00	93.00	93.00
4911	-	29	40	New Durham	Rochester	120.00	148.80	148.80
4912	-	25	-	New Durham	New Durham	240.00	297.60	297.60
4913	-	75	-	New Durham	New Durham	310.00	384.40	384.40
4914	-	79	-	New Durham	New Durham	257.00	318.68	318.68
4915	-	45	-	New Durham	Rochester	90.00	111.60	111.60

1798 DIRECT TAX

Pg/No	Occupant Surname	Occupant First Name	Owner Surname	Owner First Name	Dwg #	Val $	Expt Acr
4916	Unimproved	-	Peavey	Anthony	-	-	-
4917	Roberts	John	Roberts	John	-	-	-
4918	Runnals	Samuel	Runnals	Samuel	-	-	-
4919	-	-	Runnals	Samuel	-	-	-
4920	Saltmarsh	Thomas	Saltmarsh	Thomas	-	-	-
4921	Shaw	George	Shaw	George	1	13	-
4922	Unimproved	-	Shaw	George	-	-	-
4923	Unimproved	-	Smith	Ebenezer	-	-	-
4924	Unimproved	-	Smith	Ebenezer	-	-	-
4925	Stevens	Durrel	Stevens	Durrel	-	-	-
4926	Stewart	David	Stewart	David	-	-	-
5001	Swain	John	Swain	John	1	30	-
5002	Tash	John	Tash	John	-	-	-
5003	-	-	Tash	John	-	-	-
5004	-	-	Tash	John	-	-	-
5005	-	-	Tash	Oxford	-	-	-
5006	Tash	Thomas	Tash	Thomas	-	-	-
5007	Tash	Thomas	Tash	Thomas	-	-	-
5008	Tash	Thomas	Tash	Thomas	-	-	-
5009	Tash	Thomas	Tash	Thomas	-	-	-
5010	Unimproved	-	Tash	Thomas	-	-	-
5011	Unimproved	-	Tash	Thomas	-	-	-
5012	Unimproved	-	Tash	Thomas	-	-	-
5013	Unimproved	-	Tash	Thomas	-	-	-
5014	Unimproved	-	Tash	Thomas	-	-	-
5015	Unimproved	-	Tash	Thomas	-	-	-
5016	Unimproved	-	Tash	Thomas	-	-	-
5017	Tash	Thomas, Jr.	Tash	Thomas, Jr.	1	40	-
5018	Tash	Thomas, Jr.	Tash	Thomas, Jr.	-	-	-
5019	Taylor	Jeremiah	Taylor	Jerimiah	1	1	-
5020	Thomas	Elisha	Thomas	Elisha	1	50	-
5021	-	-	Thomas	Elisha	-	-	-
5022	Peavey	Joseph	Tibbets	Edmund	1	50	-
5023	Varney	Ebenezer	Varney	Ebenezer	1	1	-
5024	Unimproved	-	Watson	William	-	-	-
5025	Watson	Reuben	Watson	Reuben	1	40	-
5026	Wille	Benjamin	Wille	Benjamin	-	-	-
5101	Unimproved	-	Wille	David	-	-	-
5102	Unimproved	-	Wille	David	-	-	-
5103	Unimproved	-	Wille	David	-	-	-
5104	Unimproved	-	Wille	David	-	-	-
5105	Unimproved	-	Wille	David	-	-	-
5106	Wille	Joseph L.	Wille	Joseph L.	-	-	-
5107	Wille	Joseph L.	Wille	Joseph L.	-	-	-
5108	Unimproved	-	Wille	Joseph L.	-	-	-
5109	Wille	Joseph	Wille	Joseph	-	-	-
5110	Wille	Joseph, Jr.	Wille	Joseph, Jr.	-	-	-

NEW HAMPSHIRE DISTRICT 13

Pg/No	Ext Per	Acr	Per	Property Location	Residence of Owner	Value $	Eq. Val $	Total $
4916	-	49	-	New Durham	Rochester	24.50	30.38	30.38
4917	-	93	80	New Durham	New Durham	492.00	610.08	610.08
4918	-	50	-	New Durham	New Durham	250.00	310.00	-
4919	-	100	-	New Durham	New Durham	400.00	496.00	806.00
4920	-	40	-	New Durham	New Durham	120.00	148.80	148.80
4921	-	59	-	New Durham	New Durham	205.00	254.20	-
4922	-	125	-	New Durham	New Durham	125.00	155.00	409.20
4923	-	25	-	New Durham	Durham	100.00	124.00	-
4924	-	100	-	New Durham	Durham	150.00	186.00	310.00
4925	-	147	-	New Durham	New Durham	687.00	851.88	851.88
4926	-	62	80	New Durham	New Durham	62.50	77.50	77.50
5001	-	72	80	New Durham	New Durham	380.50	471.82	471.82
5002	-	200	-	New Durham	New Durham	400.00	496.00	-
5003	-	250	-	New Durham	New Durham	200.00	248.00	-
5004	-	12	-	New Durham	New Durham	24.00	29.76	773.76
5005	-	100	-	New Durham	Exeter	150.00	186.00	186.00
5006	-	70	-	New Durham	New Durham	260.00	322.40	-
5007	-	44	-	New Durham	New Durham	88.00	109.12	-
5008	-	22	-	New Durham	New Durham	44.00	54.56	-
5009	-	50	-	New Durham	New Durham	150.00	186.00	-
5010	-	50	-	New Durham	New Durham	50.00	62.00	-
5011	-	125	-	New Durham	New Durham	125.00	155.00	-
5012	-	125	-	New Durham	New Durham	125.00	155.00	-
5013	-	125	-	New Durham	New Durham	29.25	36.27	-
5014	-	125	-	New Durham	New Durham	100.00	124.00	-
5015	-	125	-	New Durham	New Durham	150.00	186.00	-
5016	-	62	80	New Durham	New Durham	62.50	77.50	1467.85
5017	-	100	-	New Durham	New Durham	370.00	458.80	-
5018	-	47	80	New Durham	New Durham	190.00	235.60	694.40
5019	-	50	-	New Durham	New Durham	260.00	322.40	322.40
5020	-	100	-	New Durham	New Durham	300.00	372.00	-
5021	-	15	-	New Durham	New Durham	15.00	18.60	390.60
5022	-	50	-	New Durham	Rochester	230.00	285.20	285.20
5023	-	125	-	New Durham	New Durham	250.00	310.00	310.00
5024	-	125	-	New Durham	New Durham	150.00	186.00	186.00
5025	-	50	-	New Durham	New Durham	200.00	248.00	248.00
5026	-	110	-	New Durham	New Durham	300.00	372.00	372.00
5101	-	125	-	New Durham	New Durham	145.00	179.80	-
5102	-	60	-	New Durham	New Durham	20.00	24.80	-
5103	-	15	-	New Durham	New Durham	15.00	18.60	-
5104	-	31	-	New Durham	New Durham	93.00	115.32	-
5105	-	49	-	New Durham	New Durham	49.00	60.76	399.28
5106	-	61	-	New Durham	New Durham	243.50	301.94	-
5107	-	125	-	New Durham	New Durham	250.00	310.00	-
5108	-	31	-	New Durham	New Durham	113.00	140.12	752.06
5109	-	100	-	New Durham	New Durham	150.00	186.00	186.00
5110	-	29	-	New Durham	New Durham	29.00	35.96	35.96

1798 DIRECT TAX

Pg/No	Occupant Surname	Occupant First Name	Owner Surname	Owner First Name	Dwg #	Val $	Expt Acr
5111	Wille	Samuel, Jr.	Wille	Samuel, Jr.	-	-	-
5112	Wille	Samuel, Jr.	Wille	Samuel, Jr.	-	-	-
5113	Unimproved	-	Wille	Samuel, Jr.	-	-	-
5114	Wille	Turner	Wille	Turner	-	-	-
5115	Nutter	Nelson	Young	Joseph	1	40	-
5116	Unimproved	-	Unknown	-	-	-	-
5117	Unimproved	-	Unknown	-	-	-	-
5118	Unimproved	-	Unknown	-	-	-	-
5119	Unimproved	-	Unknown	-	-	-	-
5120	Unimproved	-	Unknown	-	-	-	-
5121	Unimproved	-	Unknown	-	-	-	-
5122	Unimproved	-	Unknown	-	-	-	-
5123	Unimproved	-	Unknown	-	-	-	-
5124	Unimproved	-	Unknown	-	-	-	-
5125	Unimproved	-	Unknown	-	-	-	-
5126	Unimproved	-	Unknown	-	-	-	-
5201	Unimproved	-	Unknown	-	-	-	-
5202	Unimproved	-	Unknown	-	-	-	-
5203	Unimproved	-	Unknown	-	-	-	-
5204	Unimproved	-	Unknown	-	-	-	-
5205	Unimproved	-	Unknown	-	-	-	-
5206	Unimproved	-	Unknown	-	-	-	-
5207	Unimproved	-	Unknown	-	-	-	-
5208	Unimproved	-	Unknown	-	-	-	-
5209	Unimproved	-	Unknown	-	-	-	-
5210	Unimproved	-	Unknown	-	-	-	-
5211	Unimproved	-	Unknown	-	-	-	-
5212	Unimproved	-	Unknown	-	-	-	-
5213	Unimproved	-	Unknown	-	-	-	-
5214	Unimproved	-	Unknown	-	-	-	-
5215	Unimproved	-	Unknown	-	-	-	-
5216	Unimproved	-	Unknown	-	-	-	-
5217	Unimproved	-	Unknown	-	-	-	-
5218	Unimproved	-	Unknown	-	-	-	-
5219	Unimproved	-	Unknown	-	-	-	-
5220	Unimproved	-	Unknown	-	-	-	-
5221	Unimproved	-	Unknown	-	-	-	-
5222	Unimproved	-	Unknown	-	-	-	-
5223	Unimproved	-	Unknown	-	-	-	-
5224	Unimproved	-	Unknown	-	-	-	-
5225	Inhabitants	-	Public Land	-	-	-	100
5226	Inhabitants	-	Public Land	-	-	-	100
5227	Inhabitants	-	Public Land	-	-	-	125
5301	Abbot	Benjamin	Abbot	Benjamin	1	8	-
5302	Abbot	Daniel	Abbot	Daniel	-	-	-
5303	Abbot	Jedediah	Abbot	Jedediah	1	10	-
5304	Savage	Benjamin	Adams	John	1	98	-

NEW HAMPSHIRE DISTRICT 13

Pg/No	Ext Per	Acr	Per	Property Location	Residence of Owner	Value $	Eq. Val $	Total $
5111	-	61	-	New Durham	New Durham	258.00	319.92	-
5112	-	62	-	New Durham	New Durham	200.00	248.00	-
5113	-	76	-	New Durham	New Durham	200.00	248.00	815.92
5114	-	62	80	New Durham	New Durham	125.00	155.00	155.00
5115	-	100	-	New Durham	Newmarket	800.00	992.00	992.00
5116	-	100	-	New Durham	New Durham	200.00	248.00	248.00
5117	-	65	-	New Durham	New Durham	65.00	80.60	80.60
5118	-	100	-	New Durham	New Durham	100.00	124.00	124.00
5119	-	125	-	New Durham	New Durham	125.00	155.00	155.00
5120	-	100	-	New Durham	New Durham	80.00	99.20	99.20
5121	-	100	-	New Durham	New Durham	200.00	248.00	248.00
5122	-	100	-	New Durham	New Durham	150.00	186.00	186.00
5123	-	100	-	New Durham	New Durham	200.00	248.00	248.00
5124	-	122	-	New Durham	New Durham	122.00	151.28	151.28
5125	-	100	-	New Durham	New Durham	150.00	186.00	186.00
5126	-	125	-	New Durham	New Durham	125.00	155.00	155.00
5201	-	125	-	New Durham	New Durham	125.00	155.00	-
5202	-	125	-	New Durham	New Durham	200.00	248.00	-
5203	-	125	-	New Durham	New Durham	90.00	111.60	-
5204	-	125	-	New Durham	New Durham	125.00	155.00	-
5205	-	65	-	New Durham	New Durham	65.00	80.60	-
5206	-	125	-	New Durham	New Durham	31.25	38.75	-
5207	-	85	-	New Durham	New Durham	21.25	26.35	-
5208	-	125	-	New Durham	New Durham	62.50	77.50	-
5209	-	125	-	New Durham	New Durham	187.00	231.88	-
5210	-	41	-	New Durham	New Durham	82.00	101.68	-
5211	-	125	-	New Durham	New Durham	125.00	155.00	-
5212	-	59	-	New Durham	New Durham	83.75	103.85	-
5213	-	125	-	New Durham	New Durham	62.50	77.50	-
5214	-	125	-	New Durham	New Durham	31.25	38.75	-
5215	-	87	-	New Durham	New Durham	22.00	27.28	-
5216	-	125	-	New Durham	New Durham	125.00	155.00	-
5217	-	125	-	New Durham	New Durham	125.00	155.00	-
5218	-	125	-	New Durham	New Durham	125.00	155.00	-
5219	-	125	-	New Durham	New Durham	125.00	155.00	-
5220	-	125	-	New Durham	New Durham	250.00	310.00	-
5221	-	125	-	New Durham	New Durham	62.50	77.50	-
5222	-	122	-	New Durham	New Durham	122.00	151.28	-
5223	-	62	80	New Durham	New Durham	31.25	38.75	-
5224	-	125	-	New Durham	New Durham	125.00	155.00	-
5225	-	-	-	New Durham	New Durham	-	-	-
5226	-	-	-	New Durham	New Durham	-	-	-
5227	-	-	-	New Durham	New Durham	-	-	-
5301	-	30	-	Ossipee	Ossipee	60.00	74.40	74.40
5302	-	70	-	Ossipee	Ossipee	218.00	270.32	270.32
5303	-	75	-	Ossipee	Ossipee	235.00	291.40	291.40
5304	-	200	-	Ossipee	Stratham	958.00	1187.92	1187.92

1798 DIRECT TAX

Pg/No	Occupant Surname	Occupant First Name	Owner Surname	Owner First Name	Dwg #	Val $	Expt Acr
5305	Ambrose	Nathaniel	Ambrose	Nathaniel	1	20	-
5306	Beacham	Richard	Beacham	Richard	1	10	-
5307	Bickford	Joseph	Bickford	Joseph	1	10	-
5308	Blake	Sanborn	Blake	Sanborn	1	30	-
5309	Brackett	Joseph	Brackett	Joseph	1	10	-
5310	Brown	Benjamin	Brown	Benjamin	1	15	-
5311	Brown	Jacob	Brown	Jacob	-	-	-
5312	Brown	Jacob	Brown	Jacob	-	-	-
5313	Brown	Jacob	Brown	Jacob	-	-	-
5314	Brown	Jacob	Brown	Jacob	-	-	-
5315	Brown	Jacob	Brown	Jacob	-	-	-
5316	Brown	Moses	Brown	Moses	-	-	-
5317	Brown	Robert	Brown	Robert	1	15	-
5318	Brown	William	Brown	William	-	-	-
5319	Burleigh	William	Burleigh	William	1	50	-
5320	Buzzell	Joseph	Buzzell	Joseph	1	20	-
5321	-	-	Buzzell	Joseph	-	-	-
5322	Carter	Samuel	Carter	Samuel	1	10	-
5323	Carter	Stanton	Carter	Stanton	-	-	-
5324	Camey	John	Camey	John	-	-	-
5325	Chick	John	Chick	John	-	-	-
5326	Unimproved	-	Copp	David	-	-	-
5401	Cooley	John	Cooley	John	1	30	-
5402	Cooley	John	Cooley	John	0	0	-
5403	Dearborn	James	Dearborn	James	1	50	-
5404	Ames	Joseph	Dearborn	Levi	1	50	-
5405	Dearborn	Joseph	Dearborn	Joseph	1	50	-
5406	-	-	Dow	Joseph	-	-	-
5407	Demerritt	Isaac	Demerritt	Isaac	-	-	-
5408	Dodge	Jonathan	Dodge	Jonathan	-	-	-
5409	Dodge	Jonathan	Dodge	Jonathan	-	-	-
5410	Dodge	Jonathan	Dodge	Jonathan	-	-	-
5411	Dore	Benacah	Dore	Benacah	-	-	-
5412	Eldridge	Jeremiah	Eldridge	Jeremiah	-	-	-
5413	Ellis	Enoch	Ellis	Enoch	1	50	-
5414	Emerson	John	Emerson	John	1	10	-
5415	Emerson	Solomon	Emerson	Solomon	2	10	-
5416	Fogg	Joseph	Fogg	Joseph	-	-	-
5417	Fogg	Joseph, Jr.	Fogg	Joseph. Jr.	1	30	-
5418	Fogg	Seth	Fogg	Seth	-	-	-
5419	Fogg	Simon	Fogg	Simon	1	15	-
5420	Folsom	Andrew	Folsom	Andrew	-	-	-
5421	Folsom	Andrew	Folsom	Andrew	-	-	-
5422	Garland	Amos	Garland	Amos	1	20	-
5423	Garland	Joseph	Garland	Joseph	1	20	-
5424	Gilman	Benjamin	Gilman	Benjamin	1	20	-
5425	Gilman	Porter	Gilman	Porter	1	30	-

NEW HAMPSHIRE DISTRICT 13

Pg/No	Ext Per	Acr	Per	Property Location	Residence of Owner	Value $	Eq. Val $	Total $
5305	-	200	-	Ossipee	Ossipee	525.00	651.00	651.00
5306	-	100	-	Ossipee	Ossipee	550.00	682.00	682.00
5307	-	56	-	Ossipee	Ossipee	50.00	62.00	62.00
5308	-	110	-	Ossipee	Ossipee	500.00	620.00	620.00
5309	-	50	-	Ossipee	Ossipee	280.00	347.20	347.20
5310	-	66	-	Ossipee	Ossipee	75.00	93.00	93.00
5311	-	60	-	Ossipee	Ossipee	330.00	409.20	-
5312	-	150	-	Ossipee	Ossipee	400.00	496.00	-
5313	-	60	-	Ossipee	Ossipee	120.00	148.80	-
5314	-	50	-	Ossipee	Ossipee	50.00	62.00	-
5315	-	200	-	Ossipee	Ossipee	50.00	62.00	1178.00
5316	-	230	-	Ossipee	Wolfborough	800.00	992.00	992.00
5317	-	50	-	Ossipee	Ossipee	150.00	186.00	186.00
5318	-	69	-	Ossipee	Ossipee	220.00	272.80	272.80
5319	-	478	-	Ossipee	Ossipee	528.00	654.72	654.72
5320	-	50	-	Ossipee	Ossipee	300.00	372.00	-
5321	-	400	-	Ossipee	Ossipee	200.00	248.00	620.00
5322	-	40	-	Ossipee	Ossipee	50.00	62.00	62.00
5323	-	50	-	Ossipee	Ossipee	100.00	124.00	124.00
5324	-	60	-	Ossipee	Ossipee	220.00	272.80	272.80
5325	-	50	-	Ossipee	Ossipee	100.00	124.00	124.00
5326	-	400	-	Ossipee	Wakefield	400.00	496.00	496.00
5401	-	100	-	Ossipee	Ossipee	80.00	99.20	-
5402	-	100	-	Ossipee	Ossipee	50.00	62.00	161.20
5403	-	200	-	Ossipee	Ossipee	950.00	1178.00	1178.00
5404	-	250	-	Ossipee	Rochester	800.00	992.00	992.00
5405	-	90	-	Ossipee	Ossipee	500.00	620.00	620.00
5406	-	100	-	Ossipee	Hampton	300.00	372.00	372.00
5407	-	50	-	Ossipee	Ossipee	120.00	148.80	148.80
5408	-	150	-	Ossipee	Ossipee	700.00	868.00	-
5409	-	50	-	Ossipee	Ossipee	150.00	186.00	-
5410	-	100	-	Ossipee	Ossipee	100.00	124.00	1178.00
5411	-	30	-	Ossipee	Ossipee	80.00	99.20	99.20
5412	-	50	-	Ossipee	Ossipee	100.00	124.00	124.00
5413	-	235	-	Ossipee	Ossipee	300.00	372.00	372.00
5414	-	100	-	Ossipee	Ossipee	110.00	136.40	136.40
5415	-	70	-	Ossipee	Ossipee	380.00	471.20	471.20
5416	-	200	-	Ossipee	Ossipee	850.00	1054.00	1054.00
5417	-	27	-	Ossipee	Ossipee	192.00	238.08	238.08
5418	-	100	-	Ossipee	Ossipee	780.00	967.20	967.20
5419	-	50	-	Ossipee	Ossipee	300.00	372.00	372.00
5420	-	160	-	Ossipee	Ossipee	600.00	744.00	-
5421	-	100	-	Ossipee	Ossipee	150.00	186.00	930.00
5422	-	100	-	Ossipee	Ossipee	550.00	682.00	682.00
5423	-	30	-	Ossipee	Ossipee	195.00	241.80	241.80
5424	-	100	-	Ossipee	Ossipee	420.00	520.80	520.80
5425	-	125	-	Ossipee	Ossipee	700.00	868.00	868.00

1798 DIRECT TAX

Pg/No	Occupant Surname	Occupant First Name	Owner Surname	Owner First Name	Dwg #	Val $	Expt Acr
5426	Gliddon	Zebulon	Gliddon	Zebulon	1	10	-
5501	Goldsmith	Benjamin	Goldsmith	Benjamin	1	20	-
5502	Goldsmith	Hubbard	Goldsmith	Hubard	-	-	-
5503	Goldsmith	John	Goldsmith	John	1	30	-
5504	Goldsmith	John, Jr.	Goldsmith	John, Jr.	1	10	-
5505	Goudy	John	Goudy	John	1	20	-
5506	Grant	Joshua	Grant	Joshua	1	10	-
5507	Graves	Phineas	Graves	Phineas	-	-	-
5508	Unimproved	-	Goldsmith	William	-	-	-
5509	Hide	Samuel, Jr.	Hide	Samuel, Jr.	-	-	-
5510	Haley	Thomas	Haley	Thomas	1	30	-
5511	Hanson	Aaron	Hanson	Aaron	1	10	-
5512	Hanson	Moses	Hanson	Moses	1	20	-
5513	Hanson	Turner	Hanson	Turner	1	30	-
5514	Hays	Jacob	Hays	Jacob	1	30	-
5515	Hodgdon	Benjamin	Hodgdon	Benjamin	1	20	-
5516	Hodgdon	Ebenezer	Hodgdon	Ebenezer	1	15	-
5517	Hodgdon	Ichabod	Hodgdon	Ichabod	-	-	-
5518	Hodgdon	Joshua	Hodgdon	Joshua	-	-	-
5519	Hodgdon	Moses	Hodgdon	Moses	1	20	-
5520	Horsam	Ebenezer	Horsam	Ebenezer	-	-	-
5521	Horsam	Timothy	Horsam	Timothy	1	20	-
5522	Jones	David	Jones	David	-	-	-
5523	Kennison	Waldron	Kennison	Waldron	1	10	-
5524	Keys	William	Keys	William	-	-	-
5525	Keys	William	Keys	William	-	-	-
5526	Knight	Ephraim	Knight	Ephraim	-	-	-
5601	Lear	Samuel	Lear	Samuel	1	20	-
5602	Lear	Samuel, Jr.	Lear	Samuel, Jr.	1	10	-
5603	Unimproved	-	Leavitt	Joseph	-	-	-
5604	Leighton	Ephraim	Leighton	Ephraim	1	98	-
5605	Lear	William	Lear	William	-	-	-
5606	Lord	Robert	Lord	Robert	1	15	-
5607	Lord	Wentworth	Lord	Wentworth	1	25	-
5608	Mason	John	Mason	John	1	5	-
5609	Smith	Simon	Mason	John, Jr.	-	-	-
5610	Moody	Abner	Moody	Abner	1	15	-
5611	Moody	Edward	Moody	Edward	1	15	-
5612	Moody	James	Moody	James	-	-	-
5613	Moody	Jonathan	Moody	Jonathan	1	40	-
5614	Nay	Joseph	Nay	Joseph	-	-	-
5615	Nickerson	Jonathan	Nickerson	Jonathan	1	40	-
5616	Moody	Edward	Nutter	Samuel	-	-	-
5617	Nock	Drisco	Nock	Drisco	-	-	-
5618	Perkins	Thomas	Perkins	Thomas	1	40	-
5619	Unimproved	-	Peirce	John	-	-	-
5620	Unimproved	-	Peirce	John	-	-	-

NEW HAMPSHIRE DISTRICT 13

Pg/No	Ext Per	Acr	Per	Property Location	Residence of Owner	Value $	Eq. Val $	Total $
5426	-	100	-	Ossipee	Ossipee	100.00	124.00	124.00
5501	-	40	-	Ossipee	Ossipee	200.00	248.00	248.00
5502	-	60	-	Ossipee	Ossipee	200.00	248.00	248.00
5503	-	30	-	Ossipee	Ossipee	215.00	266.60	266.60
5504	-	70	-	Ossipee	Ossipee	200.00	248.00	248.00
5505	-	50	-	Ossipee	Ossipee	120.00	148.80	148.80
5506	-	50	-	Ossipee	Ossipee	110.00	136.40	136.40
5507	-	100	-	Ossipee	Ossipee	150.00	186.00	186.00
5508	-	50	-	Ossipee	Wolfborough	150.00	186.00	186.00
5509	-	50	-	Ossipee	Wolfborough	75.00	93.00	93.00
5510	-	25	-	Ossipee	Ossipee	100.00	124.00	124.00
5511	-	40	-	Ossipee	Ossipee	150.00	186.00	186.00
5512	-	86	-	Ossipee	Ossipee	208.00	257.92	257.92
5513	-	10	-	Ossipee	Ossipee	70.00	86.80	86.80
5514	-	47	-	Ossipee	Ossipee	205.00	254.20	254.20
5515	-	39	-	Ossipee	Ossipee	200.00	248.00	248.00
5516	-	200	-	Ossipee	Ossipee	355.00	440.20	440.20
5517	-	200	-	Ossipee	Ossipee	340.00	421.60	421.60
5518	-	123	-	Ossipee	Ossipee	250.00	310.00	310.00
5519	-	88	-	Ossipee	Ossipee	260.00	322.40	322.40
5520	-	62	-	Ossipee	Ossipee	150.00	186.00	186.00
5521	-	80	-	Ossipee	Ossipee	260.00	322.40	322.40
5522	-	64	-	Ossipee	Ossipee	200.00	248.00	248.00
5523	-	50	-	Ossipee	Ossipee	60.00	74.40	74.40
5524	-	25	-	Ossipee	Ossipee	100.00	124.00	-
5525	-	80	-	Ossipee	Ossipee	80.00	99.20	223.20
5526	-	100	-	Ossipee	Ossipee	420.00	520.80	520.80
5601	-	100	-	Ossipee	Ossipee	120.00	148.80	148.80
5602	-	100	-	Ossipee	Ossipee	260.00	322.40	322.40
5603	-	400	-	Ossipee	Wakefield	200.00	248.00	248.00
5604	-	175	-	Ossipee	Ossipee	700.00	868.00	868.00
5605	-	25	-	Ossipee	Ossipee	75.00	93.00	93.00
5606	-	45	-	Ossipee	Ossipee	100.00	124.00	124.00
5607	-	50	-	Ossipee	Ossipee	115.00	142.60	142.60
5608	-	50	-	Ossipee	Ossipee	295.00	365.80	365.80
5609	-	80	-	Ossipee	Penobscot	80.00	99.20	99.20
5610	-	-	-	Ossipee	Ossipee	15.00	18.60	18.60
5611	-	78	-	Ossipee	Ossipee	300.00	372.00	372.00
5612	-	50	-	Ossipee	Ossipee	50.00	62.00	62.00
5613	-	50	-	Ossipee	Ossipee	300.00	372.00	372.00
5614	-	100	-	Ossipee	Ossipee	640.00	793.60	793.60
5615	-	100	-	Ossipee	Ossipee	240.00	297.60	297.60
5616	-	12	-	Ossipee	Portsmouth	72.00	89.28	89.28
5617	-	30	-	Ossipee	Ossipee	80.00	99.20	99.20
5618	-	50	-	Ossipee	Ossipee	300.00	372.00	372.00
5619	-	400	-	Ossipee	Portsmouth	200.00	248.00	-
5620	-	400	-	Ossipee	Portsmouth	100.00	124.00	372.00

1798 DIRECT TAX

Pg/No	Occupant Surname	Occupant First Name	Owner Surname	Owner First Name	Dwg #	Val $	Expt Acr
5621	Pitman	Joseph	Pitman	Joseph	1	10	-
5622	Poland	Josiah	Poland	Josiah	-	-	-
5623	Poland	Josiah	Poland	Josiah	-	-	-
5624	Prebble	Benjamin	Prebble	Benjamin	1	30	-
5625	Quarles	Samuel	Quarles	Samuel	-	-	-
5626	Roberts	Daniel	Roberts	Daniel	1	10	-
5701	Roberts	James	Roberts	James	-	-	-
5702	Roberts	James, Jr.	Roberts	James, Jr.	-	-	-
5703	Roberts	Moses	Roberts	Moses	1	20	-
5704	Roberts	Moses	Roberts	Moses	-	-	-
5705	Roles	Samuel	Roles	Samuel	1	25	-
5706	Rogers	Thomas	Rogers	Thomas	-	-	-
5707	Sanderson	John	Sanderson	John	1	25	-
5708	Siedgal	Benjamin, Jr.	Siedgal	Benjamin, Jr.	1	40	-
5709	Siedgal	John	Siedgal	John	1	10	-
5710	Siedgal	John, Jr.	Siedgal	John, Jr.	-	-	-
5711	Sias	Eliphalet	Sias	Eliph't	-	-	-
5712	-	-	Sias	Eliph't	-	-	-
5713	Sias	Samuel, Jr.	Sias	Samuel, Jr.	1	25	-
5714	Smart	Robert	Smart	Robert	1	40	-
5715	Smart	Winthrop	Smart	Winthrop	1	40	-
5716	Smith	Daniel	Smith	Daniel	1	35	-
5717	-	-	Smith	Jaboz	-	-	-
5718	Smith	Samuel	Smith	Samuel	-	-	-
5719	Staple	George	Staple	George	1	75	-
5720	Tasker	Samuel	Tasker	Samuel	1	30	-
5721	Tasker	Stephen	Tasker	Stephen	-	-	-
5722	Taylor	Benjamin	Taylor	Benjamin	1	10	-
5723	Thing	Winthrop	Thing	Winthrop	-	-	-
5724	Thing	Zebedee	Thing	Zebedee	1	20	-
5725	Towle	Josiah	Towle	Josiah	1	35	-
5726	Tucker	John	Tucker	John	-	-	-
5801	Tucker	Samuel	Tucker	Samuel	1	15	-
5802	Welch	John	Welch	John	-	-	-
5803	Wentworth	Stephen	Wentworth	Stephen	-	-	-
5804	White	Silas	White	Silas	-	-	-
5805	Young	John	Young	John	-	-	-
5806	-	-	Young	John	-	-	-
5807	Young	Moses	Young	Moses	-	-	-
5808	Unimproved	-	Unknown	-	-	-	-
5809	Unimproved	-	Unknown	-	-	-	-
5810	Unimproved	-	Unknown	-	-	-	-
5811	Unimproved	-	Unknown	-	-	-	-
5812	Unimproved	-	Unknown	-	-	-	-
5813	Unimproved	-	Unknown	-	-	-	-
5814	Unimproved	-	Unknown	-	-	-	-
5815	Unimproved	-	Unknown	-	-	-	-

NEW HAMPSHIRE DISTRICT 13

Pg/ No	Ext Per	Acr	Per	Property Location	Residence of Owner	Value $	Eq. Val $	Total $
5621	-	140	-	Ossipee	Ossipee	450.00	558.00	558.00
5622	-	100	-	Ossipee	Ossipee	630.00	781.20	-
5623	-	94	-	Ossipee	Ossipee	600.00	744.00	1525.20
5624	-	80	-	Ossipee	Ossipee	350.00	434.00	434.00
5625	-	50	-	Ossipee	Ossipee	150.00	186.00	186.00
5626	-	100	-	Ossipee	Ossipee	300.00	372.00	372.00
5701	-	52	-	Ossipee	Ossipee	200.00	248.00	248.00
5702	-	100	-	Ossipee	Ossipee	100.00	124.00	124.00
5703	-	66	-	Ossipee	Ossipee	300.00	372.00	-
5704	-	50	-	Ossipee	Ossipee	150.00	186.00	558.00
5705	-	100	-	Ossipee	Ossipee	500.00	620.00	620.00
5706	-	55	-	Ossipee	Ossipee	220.00	272.80	272.80
5707	-	40	-	Ossipee	Ossipee	65.00	80.60	80.60
5708	-	140	-	Ossipee	Ossipee	600.00	744.00	744.00
5709	-	40	-	Ossipee	Ossipee	120.00	148.80	148.80
5710	-	20	-	Ossipee	Ossipee	60.00	74.40	74.40
5711	-	100	-	Ossipee	Ossipee	300.00	372.00	-
5712	-	13	-	Ossipee	Ossipee	39.00	48.36	420.36
5713	-	100	-	Ossipee	Ossipee	180.00	223.20	223.20
5714	-	50	-	Ossipee	Ossipee	150.00	186.00	186.00
5715	-	100	-	Ossipee	Ossipee	400.00	496.00	496.00
5716	-	400	-	Ossipee	Ossipee	800.00	992.00	992.00
5717	-	100	-	Ossipee	Brintwood	100.00	124.00	124.00
5718	-	105	-	Ossipee	Ossipee	550.00	682.00	682.00
5719	-	25	-	Ossipee	Ossipee	200.00	248.00	248.00
5720	-	200	-	Ossipee	Ossipee	450.00	558.00	558.00
5721	-	60	-	Ossipee	Ossipee	120.00	148.80	148.80
5722	-	44	-	Ossipee	Ossipee	100.00	124.00	124.00
5723	-	10	-	Ossipee	Tuftonboro	30.00	37.20	37.20
5724	-	40	-	Ossipee	Ossipee	120.00	148.80	148.80
5725	-	50	-	Ossipee	Ossipee	100.00	124.00	124.00
5726	-	50	-	Ossipee	Ossipee	125.00	155.00	155.00
5801	-	50	-	Ossipee	Ossipee	150.00	186.00	186.00
5802	-	109	-	Ossipee	Ossipee	218.00	270.32	270.32
5803	-	60	-	Ossipee	Ossipee	90.00	111.60	111.60
5804	-	100	-	Ossipee	Ossipee	50.00	62.00	62.00
5805	-	100	-	Ossipee	Ossipee	650.00	806.00	-
5806	-	100	-	Ossipee	Ossipee	250.00	310.00	1116.00
5807	-	50	-	Ossipee	Ossipee	100.00	124.00	124.00
5808	-	100	-	Ossipee	Ossipee	300.00	372.00	372.00
5809	-	400	-	Ossipee	Ossipee	200.00	248.00	248.00
5810	-	400	-	Ossipee	Ossipee	300.00	372.00	372.00
5811	-	400	-	Ossipee	Ossipee	200.00	248.00	248.00
5812	-	400	-	Ossipee	Ossipee	250.00	310.00	310.00
5813	-	200	-	Ossipee	Ossipee	200.00	248.00	248.00
5814	-	300	-	Ossipee	Ossipee	150.00	186.00	186.00
5815	-	200	-	Ossipee	Ossipee	300.00	372.00	372.00

1798 DIRECT TAX

Pg/No	Occupant Surname	Occupant First Name	Owner Surname	Owner First Name	Dwg #	Val $	Expt Acr
5816	Unimproved	-	Unknown	-	-	-	-
5817	Unimproved	-	Unknown	-	-	-	-
5818	Unimproved	-	Unknown	-	-	-	-
5819	Unimproved	-	Unknown	-	-	-	-
5820	Unimproved	-	Unknown	-	-	-	-
5821	Unimproved	-	Unknown	-	-	-	-
5822	Unimproved	-	Unknown	-	-	-	-
5823	Unimproved	-	Unknown	-	-	-	-
5824	Unimproved	-	Unknown	-	-	-	-
5825	Unimproved	-	Unknown	-	-	-	-
5826	Unimproved	-	Unknown	-	-	-	-
5901	Unimproved	-	Unknown	-	-	-	-
5902	Unimproved	-	Unknown	-	-	-	-
5903	Unimproved	-	Unknown	-	-	-	-
5904	Unimproved	-	Unknown	-	-	-	-
5905	Unimproved	-	Unknown	-	-	-	-
5906	Unimproved	-	Unknown	-	-	-	-
5907	Unimproved	-	Unknown	-	-	-	-
5908	Unimproved	-	Unknown	-	-	-	-
5909	Unimproved	-	Unknown	-	-	-	-
5910	Unimproved	-	Unknown	-	-	-	-
5911	Unimproved	-	Unknown	-	-	-	-
5912	Kennison	John	Unknown	-	-	-	-
5913	Kennison	John, Jr.	Unknown	-	-	-	-
5914	Unimproved	-	Unknown	-	-	-	-
5915	Unimproved	-	Unknown	-	-	-	-
5916	Unimproved	-	Unknown	-	-	-	-
5917	Unimproved	-	Unknown	-	-	-	-
5918	Unimproved	-	Unknown	-	-	-	-
5919	Unimproved	-	Unknown	-	-	-	-
5920	Unimproved	-	Unknown	-	-	-	-
5921	Unimproved	-	Unknown	-	-	-	-
5922	Unimproved	-	Unknown	-	-	-	-
5923	Unimproved	-	Unknown	-	-	-	-
5924	Unimproved	-	Unknown	-	-	-	-
5925	Unimproved	-	Unknown	-	-	-	-
5926	Unimproved	-	Unknown	-	-	-	-
6001	Unimproved	-	Unknown	-	-	-	-
6002	Unimproved	-	Unknown	-	-	-	-
6003	Unimproved	-	Unknown	-	-	-	-
6004	Unimproved	-	Unknown	-	-	-	-
6005	Unimproved	-	Unknown	-	-	-	-
6006	Unimproved	-	Unknown	-	-	-	-
6007	Unimproved	-	Unknown	-	-	-	-
6008	Unimproved	-	Unknown	-	-	-	-
6009	Unimproved	-	Unknown	-	-	-	-
6010	Unimproved	-	Unknown	-	-	-	-

NEW HAMPSHIRE DISTRICT 13

Pg/No	Ext Per	Acr	Per	Property Location	Residence of Owner	Value $	Eq. Val $	Total $
5816	-	400	-	Ossipee	Ossipee	200.00	248.00	248.00
5817	-	400	-	Ossipee	Ossipee	200.00	248.00	248.00
5818	-	400	-	Ossipee	Ossipee	300.00	372.00	372.00
5819	-	400	-	Ossipee	Ossipee	200.00	248.00	248.00
5820	-	400	-	Ossipee	Ossipee	300.00	372.00	372.00
5821	-	400	-	Ossipee	Ossipee	200.00	248.00	248.00
5822	-	400	-	Ossipee	Ossipee	200.00	248.00	248.00
5823	-	400	-	Ossipee	Ossipee	200.00	248.00	248.00
5824	-	400	-	Ossipee	Ossipee	100.00	124.00	124.00
5825	-	400	-	Ossipee	Ossipee	200.00	248.00	248.00
5826	-	400	-	Ossipee	Ossipee	200.00	248.00	248.00
5901	-	400	-	Ossipee	Ossipee	150.00	186.00	-
5902	-	400	-	Ossipee	Ossipee	200.00	248.00	-
5903	-	400	-	Ossipee	Ossipee	300.00	372.00	-
5904	-	400	-	Ossipee	Ossipee	600.00	744.00	-
5905	-	200	-	Ossipee	Ossipee	300.00	372.00	-
5906	-	400	-	Ossipee	Ossipee	200.00	248.00	-
5907	-	400	-	Ossipee	Ossipee	200.00	248.00	-
5908	-	400	-	Ossipee	Ossipee	200.00	248.00	-
5909	-	400	-	Ossipee	Ossipee	800.00	992.00	-
5910	-	400	-	Ossipee	Ossipee	200.00	248.00	-
5911	-	400	-	Ossipee	Ossipee	200.00	248.00	-
5912	-	100	-	Ossipee	Ossipee	200.00	248.00	-
5913	-	100	-	Ossipee	Ossipee	200.00	248.00	-
5914	-	100	-	Ossipee	Ossipee	50.00	62.00	-
5915	-	100	-	Ossipee	Ossipee	50.00	62.00	-
5916	-	100	-	Ossipee	Ossipee	50.00	62.00	-
5917	-	100	-	Ossipee	Ossipee	50.00	62.00	-
5918	-	100	-	Ossipee	Ossipee	50.00	62.00	-
5919	-	100	-	Ossipee	Ossipee	50.00	62.00	-
5920	-	100	-	Ossipee	Ossipee	50.00	62.00	-
5921	-	100	-	Ossipee	Ossipee	50.00	62.00	-
5922	-	100	-	Ossipee	Ossipee	50.00	62.00	-
5923	-	100	-	Ossipee	Ossipee	50.00	62.00	-
5924	-	100	-	Ossipee	Ossipee	50.00	62.00	-
5925	-	100	-	Ossipee	Ossipee	50.00	62.00	-
5926	-	100	-	Ossipee	Ossipee	50.00	62.00	-
6001	-	100	-	Ossipee	Ossipee	50.00	62.00	62.00
6002	-	100	-	Ossipee	Ossipee	50.00	62.00	62.00
6003	-	100	-	Ossipee	Ossipee	50.00	62.00	62.00
6004	-	100	-	Ossipee	Ossipee	50.00	62.00	62.00
6005	-	100	-	Ossipee	Ossipee	50.00	62.00	62.00
6006	-	100	-	Ossipee	Ossipee	50.00	62.00	62.00
6007	-	100	-	Ossipee	Ossipee	50.00	62.00	62.00
6008	-	100	-	Ossipee	Ossipee	50.00	62.00	62.00
6009	-	100	-	Ossipee	Ossipee	50.00	62.00	62.00
6010	-	100	-	Ossipee	Ossipee	50.00	62.00	62.00

1798 DIRECT TAX

Pg/No	Occupant Surname	Occupant First Name	Owner Surname	Owner First Name	Dwg #	Val $	Expt Acr
6011	Unimproved	-	Unknown	-	-	-	-
6012	Unimproved	-	Unknown	-	-	-	-
6013	Unimproved	-	Unknown	-	-	-	-
6014	Unimproved	-	Unknown	-	-	-	-
6015	Unimproved	-	Unknown	-	-	-	-
6016	Unimproved	-	Unknown	-	-	-	-
6017	Unimproved	-	Unknown	-	-	-	-
6018	Unimproved	-	Unknown	-	-	-	-
6019	Unimproved	-	Unknown	-	-	-	-
6020	Unimproved	-	Unknown	-	-	-	-
6021	Unimproved	-	Unknown	-	-	-	-
6022	Unimproved	-	Unknown	-	-	-	-
6023	Unimproved	-	Unknown	-	-	-	-
6024	Unimproved	-	Unknown	-	-	-	-
6025	Unimproved	-	Unknown	-	-	-	-
6026	Unimproved	-	Unknown	-	-	-	-
6101	Unimproved	-	Unknown	-	-	-	-
6102	Unimproved	-	Unknown	-	-	-	-
6103	Unimproved	-	Unknown	-	-	-	-
6104	Unimproved	-	Unknown	-	-	-	-
6105	Unimproved	-	Unknown	-	-	-	-
6106	Unimproved	-	Unknown	-	-	-	-
6107	Unimproved	-	Unknown	-	-	-	-
6108	Unimproved	-	Unknown	-	-	-	-
6109	Unimproved	-	Unknown	-	-	-	-
6110	Unimproved	-	Unknown	-	-	-	-
6111	Unimproved	-	Unknown	-	-	-	-
6112	Unimproved	-	Unknown	-	-	-	-
6113	Unimproved	-	Unknown	-	-	-	-
6114	Unimproved	-	Unknown	-	-	-	-
6115	Unimproved	-	Unknown	-	-	-	-
6116	Unimproved	-	Unknown	-	-	-	-
6117	Unimproved	-	Unknown	-	-	-	-
6118	Unimproved	-	Unknown	-	-	-	-
6119	Unimproved	-	Unknown	-	-	-	-
6120	Unimproved	-	Unknown	-	-	-	-
6121	Unimproved	-	Unknown	-	-	-	-
6122	Unimproved	-	Unknown	-	-	-	-
6123	Unimproved	-	Unknown	-	-	-	-
6124	Unimproved	-	Unknown	-	-	-	-
6125	Unimproved	-	Unknown	-	-	-	-
6126	Unimproved	-	Unknown	-	-	-	-
6201	Unimproved	-	Unknown	-	-	-	-
6202	Unimproved	-	Unknown	-	-	-	-
6203	Unimproved	-	Unknown	-	-	-	-
6204	Unimproved	-	Unknown	-	-	-	-
6205	Unimproved	-	Unknown	-	-	-	-

NEW HAMPSHIRE DISTRICT 13

Pg/No	Ext Per	Acr	Per	Property Location	Residence of Owner	Value $	Eq. Val $	Total $
6011	-	100	-	Ossipee	Ossipee	50.00	62.00	62.00
6012	-	100	-	Ossipee	Ossipee	50.00	62.00	62.00
6013	-	100	-	Ossipee	Ossipee	50.00	62.00	62.00
6014	-	100	-	Ossipee	Ossipee	50.00	62.00	62.00
6015	-	100	-	Ossipee	Ossipee	50.00	62.00	62.00
6016	-	100	-	Ossipee	Ossipee	50.00	62.00	62.00
6017	-	100	-	Ossipee	Ossipee	50.00	62.00	62.00
6018	-	100	-	Ossipee	Ossipee	50.00	62.00	62.00
6019	-	100	-	Ossipee	Ossipee	50.00	62.00	62.00
6020	-	100	-	Ossipee	Ossipee	50.00	62.00	62.00
6021	-	100	-	Ossipee	Ossipee	50.00	62.00	62.00
6022	-	100	-	Ossipee	Ossipee	50.00	62.00	62.00
6023	-	100	-	Ossipee	Ossipee	50.00	62.00	62.00
6024	-	100	-	Ossipee	Ossipee	50.00	62.00	62.00
6025	-	100	-	Ossipee	Ossipee	50.00	62.00	62.00
6026	-	100	-	Ossipee	Ossipee	50.00	62.00	62.00
6101	-	100	-	Ossipee	Ossipee	50.00	62.00	62.00
6102	-	100	-	Ossipee	Ossipee	50.00	62.00	62.00
6103	-	100	-	Ossipee	Ossipee	50.00	62.00	62.00
6104	-	100	-	Ossipee	Ossipee	50.00	62.00	62.00
6105	-	100	-	Ossipee	Ossipee	50.00	62.00	62.00
6106	-	100	-	Ossipee	Ossipee	50.00	62.00	62.00
6107	-	100	-	Ossipee	Ossipee	50.00	62.00	62.00
6108	-	100	-	Ossipee	Ossipee	50.00	62.00	62.00
6109	-	100	-	Ossipee	Ossipee	50.00	62.00	62.00
6110	-	100	-	Ossipee	Ossipee	50.00	62.00	62.00
6111	-	100	-	Ossipee	Ossipee	50.00	62.00	62.00
6112	-	100	-	Ossipee	Ossipee	50.00	62.00	62.00
6113	-	100	-	Ossipee	Ossipee	50.00	62.00	62.00
6114	-	100	-	Ossipee	Ossipee	50.00	62.00	62.00
6115	-	100	-	Ossipee	Ossipee	50.00	62.00	62.00
6116	-	100	-	Ossipee	Ossipee	50.00	62.00	62.00
6117	-	100	-	Ossipee	Ossipee	50.00	62.00	62.00
6118	-	100	-	Ossipee	Ossipee	50.00	62.00	62.00
6119	-	100	-	Ossipee	Ossipee	50.00	62.00	62.00
6120	-	100	-	Ossipee	Ossipee	50.00	62.00	62.00
6121	-	100	-	Ossipee	Ossipee	50.00	62.00	62.00
6122	-	100	-	Ossipee	Ossipee	50.00	62.00	62.00
6123	-	100	-	Ossipee	Ossipee	50.00	62.00	62.00
6124	-	100	-	Ossipee	Ossipee	50.00	62.00	62.00
6125	-	100	-	Ossipee	Ossipee	50.00	62.00	62.00
6126	-	100	-	Ossipee	Ossipee	50.00	62.00	62.00
6201	-	100	-	Ossipee	Ossipee	50.00	62.00	62.00
6202	-	100	-	Ossipee	Ossipee	50.00	62.00	62.00
6203	-	100	-	Ossipee	Ossipee	50.00	62.00	62.00
6204	-	100	-	Ossipee	Ossipee	50.00	62.00	62.00
6205	-	100	-	Ossipee	Ossipee	50.00	62.00	62.00

1798 DIRECT TAX

Pg/No	Occupant Surname	Occupant First Name	Owner Surname	Owner First Name	Dwg #	Val $	Expt Acr
6206	Unimproved	-	Unknown	-	-	-	-
6207	Unimproved	-	Unknown	-	-	-	-
6208	Unimproved	-	Unknown	-	-	-	-
6209	Unimproved	-	Unknown	-	-	-	-
6210	Unimproved	-	Unknown	-	-	-	-
6211	Unimproved	-	Unknown	-	-	-	-
6212	Unimproved	-	Unknown	-	-	-	-
6213	Unimproved	-	Unknown	-	-	-	-
6214	Unimproved	-	Unknown	-	-	-	-
6215	Unimproved	-	Unknown	-	-	-	-
6216	Unimproved	-	Unknown	-	-	-	-
6217	Unimproved	-	Unknown	-	-	-	-
6218	Unimproved	-	Unknown	-	-	-	-
6219	Unimproved	-	Unknown	-	-	-	-
6220	Unimproved	-	Unknown	-	-	-	-
6221	Unimproved	-	Unknown	-	-	-	-
6222	Unimproved	-	Unknown	-	-	-	-
6223	Unimproved	-	Unknown	-	-	-	-
6224	Unimproved	-	Unknown	-	-	-	-
6225	Unimproved	-	Unknown	-	-	-	-
6226	Unimproved	-	Unknown	-	-	-	-
6301	Unimproved	-	Unknown	-	-	-	-
6302	Unimproved	-	Unknown	-	-	-	-
6303	Unimproved	-	Unknown	-	-	-	-
6304	Unimproved	-	Unknown	-	-	-	-
6305	Unimproved	-	Unknown	-	-	-	-
6306	Unimproved	-	Unknown	-	-	-	-
6307	Bean	Joel	Bean	Joel	-	-	-
6308	Bean	Joel	Bean	Joel	-	-	-
6309	Bennet	Benjamin	Bennet	Benjamin	-	-	-
6310	Bennet	Thomas	Bennet	Thomas	1	48	-
6311	Brown	Ephraim	Brown	Ephraim	1	64	-
6312	Buzzell	Joseph	Buzzell	Joseph	-	-	-
6313	Buzzell	Joseph, Jr.	Buzzell	Joseph, Jr.	-	-	-
6314	Buzzell	Ithamar	Buzzell	Ithamar	-	-	-
6315	Buzzell	Silas	Buzzell	Silas	-	-	-
6316	Clough	Simon	Clough	Simon	-	-	-
6317	Unimproved	-	Clough	Simon	-	-	-
6318	Carr	Archelaus	Carr	Archelaus	-	-	-
6319	Chamberlin	Ephraim	Chamberlin	Ephraim	-	-	-
6320	Chamberlin	Ephraim, Jr.	Chamberlin	Ephraim, Jr.	1	48	-
6321	Chamberlin	Jacob	Chamberlin	Jacob	-	-	-
6322	Unimproved	-	Chamberlin	Jacob	-	-	-
6323	Chamberlin	Joseph	Chamberlin	Joseph	1	56	-
6324	Chamberlin	Paul	Chamberlin	Paul	-	-	-
6325	Clements	Enoch	Clements	Enoch	1	8	-
6326	Clements	Job	Clements	Job	-	-	-

NEW HAMPSHIRE DISTRICT 13

Pg/No	Ext Per	Acr	Per	Property Location	Residence of Owner	Value $	Eq. Val $	Total $
6206	-	100	-	Ossipee	Ossipee	50.00	62.00	62.00
6207	-	100	-	Ossipee	Ossipee	50.00	62.00	62.00
6208	-	100	-	Ossipee	Ossipee	50.00	62.00	62.00
6209	-	100	-	Ossipee	Ossipee	50.00	62.00	62.00
6210	-	100	-	Ossipee	Ossipee	50.00	62.00	62.00
6211	-	100	-	Ossipee	Ossipee	50.00	62.00	62.00
6212	-	100	-	Ossipee	Ossipee	50.00	62.00	62.00
6213	-	100	-	Ossipee	Ossipee	50.00	62.00	62.00
6214	-	100	-	Ossipee	Ossipee	50.00	62.00	62.00
6215	-	100	-	Ossipee	Ossipee	50.00	62.00	62.00
6216	-	100	-	Ossipee	Ossipee	50.00	62.00	62.00
6217	-	100	-	Ossipee	Ossipee	50.00	62.00	62.00
6218	-	100	-	Ossipee	Ossipee	50.00	62.00	62.00
6219	-	100	-	Ossipee	Ossipee	50.00	62.00	62.00
6220	-	100	-	Ossipee	Ossipee	50.00	62.00	62.00
6221	-	100	-	Ossipee	Ossipee	50.00	62.00	62.00
6222	-	100	-	Ossipee	Ossipee	50.00	62.00	62.00
6223	-	100	-	Ossipee	Ossipee	50.00	62.00	62.00
6224	-	100	-	Ossipee	Ossipee	50.00	62.00	62.00
6225	-	100	-	Ossipee	Ossipee	50.00	62.00	62.00
6226	-	100	-	Ossipee	Ossipee	50.00	62.00	62.00
6301	-	100	-	Ossipee	Ossipee	50.00	62.00	62.00
6302	-	100	-	Ossipee	Ossipee	50.00	62.00	62.00
6303	-	100	-	Ossipee	Ossipee	50.00	62.00	62.00
6304	-	100	-	Ossipee	Ossipee	50.00	62.00	62.00
6305	-	100	-	Ossipee	Ossipee	50.00	62.00	62.00
6306	-	100	-	Ossipee	Ossipee	50.00	62.00	62.00
6307	-	59	-	Alton	Alton	382.40	474.18	-
6308	-	159	-	Alton	Alton	381.60	473.18	947.36
6309	-	106	-	Alton	Alton	572.80	710.27	-
6310	-	40	-	Alton	Alton	224.00	277.76	-
6311	-	100	-	Alton	Alton	280.00	347.20	-
6312	-	99	80	Alton	Alton	400.00	496.00	-
6313	-	75	-	Alton	Alton	184.00	228.16	-
6314	-	50	-	Alton	Alton	80.00	99.20	-
6315	-	75	-	Alton	Alton	320.00	396.80	2555.30
6316	-	230	-	Alton	Alton	600.00	744.00	-
6317	-	69	-	Alton	Alton	80.00	99.20	843.20
6318	-	30	-	Alton	Alton	96.00	119.04	119.04
6319	-	98	-	Alton	Alton	600.00	744.00	744.00
6320	-	200	-	Alton	Alton	800.00	992.00	992.00
6321	-	139	-	Alton	Alton	699.20	867.01	-
6322	-	100	-	Alton	Alton	80.00	99.20	966.21
6323	-	125	-	Alton	Alton	696.00	863.04	863.04
6324	-	74	120	Alton	Alton	400.00	496.00	496.00
6325	-	55	80	Alton	Alton	184.00	228.16	228.16
6326	-	60	-	Alton	Alton	240.00	297.60	297.60

1798 DIRECT TAX

Pg/No	Occupant Surname	Occupant First Name	Owner Surname	Owner First Name	Dwg #	Val $	Expt Acr
6401	Clough	Aaron	Clough	Aaron	1	32	-
6402	Unimproved	-	Clough	Isaac S.	-	-	-
6403	-	-	Clough	Simon	-	-	-
6404	Clough	Perley	Clough	Perley	-	-	-
6405	Clough	Samuel	Clough	Samuel	-	-	-
6406	Coffin	Jonathan	Coffin	Jonathan	-	-	-
6407	Coffin	Jonathan	Coffin	Jonathan	-	-	-
6408	Young	Joseph	Coffin	Jonathan	-	-	-
6409	Unimproved	-	Cogswell	Thomas	-	-	-
6410	Unimproved	-	Cogswell	Thomas	-	-	-
6411	Unimproved	-	Cogswell	Thomas	-	-	-
6412	Unimproved	-	Cogswell	Thomas	-	-	-
6413	Unimproved	-	Cogswell	Thomas	-	-	-
6414	Unimproved	-	Cogswell	Thomas	-	-	-
6415	Davis	Eleazer	Davis	Eleazer	-	-	-
6416	Davis	Gideon	Davis	Gideon	-	-	-
6417	Pinkham	Stephen	Davis	Gideon	-	-	-
6418	Davis	Hezekiah	Davis	Hezekiah	-	-	-
6419	Davis	Nathaniel	Davis	Nathaniel	-	-	-
6420	Davis	Timothy	Davis	Timothy	-	-	-
6421	Unimproved	-	Davis	Timothy	-	-	-
6422	Davis	Zebulon	Davis	Zebulon	-	-	-
6423	Davis	Zebulon	Davis	Zebulon	-	-	-
6424	Dudley	Daniel	Dudley	Daniel	-	-	-
6425	Unimproved	-	Dudley	Daniel	-	-	-
6426	Dudley	Stephen	Dudley	Stephen	-	-	-
6427	-	-	Dudley	Stephen	-	-	-
6501	-	-	Dutton	Thomas	-	-	-
6502	-	-	Eaton	Joshua	-	-	-
6503	Edgerly	Benjamin	Edgerly	Benjamin	1	24	-
6504	Edgerly	Thomas	Edgerly	Thomas	-	-	-
6505	Elkins	Samuel	Elkins	Samuel	-	-	-
6506	-	-	Evans	Stephen	-	-	-
6507	Folsom	John	Folsom	John	-	-	-
6508	Flanders	Thomas	Flanders	Thomas	-	-	-
6509	Flanders	Thomas	Flanders	Thomas	-	-	-
6510	Flanders	Ezekiel	Flanders	Ezekiel	-	-	-
6511	Flanders	Ezekiel	Flanders	Ezekiel	-	-	-
6512	Flanders	Ezekiel, Jr.	Flanders	Ezekiel, Jr.	-	-	-
6513	Flanders	Richard	Flanders	Richard	-	-	-
6514	Clough	Samuel	Fisher	John	-	-	-
6515	Fall	Stephen	Fall	Stephen	1	-	-
6516	Page	John	French	Benjamin	1	-	-
6517	French	Ebenezer	French	Ebenezer	1	-	-
6518	Gilman	Moses	Gilman	Moses	-	-	-
6519	Bean	Peter	Gilman	Moses	1	-	-
6520	-	-	Gilman	Moses	-	-	-

NEW HAMPSHIRE DISTRICT 13

Pg/No	Ext Per	Acr	Per	Property Location	Residence of Owner	Value $	Eq. Val $	Total $
6401	-	60	-	Alton	Alton	256.00	317.44	317.44
6402	-	122	-	Alton	Alton	390.40	484.10	484.10
6403	-	1	-	Alton	Gilmanton	32.00	39.68	39.68
6404	-	99	120	Alton	Alton	320.00	396.80	396.80
6405	-	122	-	Alton	Alton	360.00	446.40	446.40
6406	-	99	-	Alton	Alton	634.40	786.66	-
6407	-	100	-	Alton	Alton	160.00	198.40	-
6408	-	200	-	Alton	Alton	552.00	684.48	1669.54
6409	-	100	-	Alton	Gilmanton	40.00	49.60	-
6410	-	490	-	Alton	Gilmanton	261.00	323.64	-
6411	-	125	-	Alton	Gilmanton	67.20	83.32	-
6412	-	200	-	Alton	Gilmanton	80.00	99.20	-
6413	-	212	-	Alton	Gilmanton	169.60	210.30	-
6414	-	80	-	Alton	Gilmanton	42.40	52.58	818.64
6415	-	398	-	Alton	Alton	2332.80	2892.67	2892.67
6416	-	149	-	Alton	Alton	784.00	972.16	-
6417	-	149	-	Alton	Alton	752.00	932.48	1904.64
6418	-	150	-	Alton	Alton	720.00	892.80	892.80
6419	-	150	-	Alton	Alton	480.00	595.20	595.20
6420	-	170	-	Alton	Alton	824.00	1021.76	-
6421	-	200	-	Alton	Alton	40.00	49.60	1071.36
6422	-	148	-	Alton	Alton	794.40	985.06	-
6423	-	50	-	Alton	Alton	240.00	297.60	1282.66
6424	-	168	-	Alton	Alton	835.20	1035.65	-
6425	-	100	-	Alton	Alton	160.00	198.40	1234.05
6426	-	150	-	Alton	Alton	772.00	957.28	-
6427	-	100	-	Alton	Alton	160.00	198.40	1155.68
6501	-	100	-	Alton	Alton	160.00	198.40	198.40
6502	-	100	-	Alton	Gilmanton	160.00	198.40	198.40
6503	-	75	-	Alton	Alton	240.00	297.60	297.40
6504	-	47	-	Alton	Alton	160.00	198.40	198.40
6505	-	40	-	Alton	Alton	128.00	158.72	158.72
6506	-	250	-	Alton	Dover	100.00	124.00	124.00
6507	-	99	80	Alton	Alton	320.00	396.80	396.80
6508	-	99	-	Alton	Alton	480.00	595.20	-
6509	-	86	-	Alton	Alton	68.80	85.31	680.51
6510	-	39	-	Alton	Alton	219.20	271.81	-
6511	-	100	-	Alton	Alton	160.00	198.40	470.21
6512	-	50	-	Alton	Alton	208.00	257.92	257.92
6513	-	50	-	Alton	Alton	240.00	297.60	297.60
6514	-	300	-	Alton	London, GB	1080.00	1339.20	1339.20
6515	-	50	-	Alton	Alton	240.00	297.60	297.60
6516	-	170	-	Alton	Gilmanton	752.00	932.48	932.48
6517	-	40	-	Alton	Alton	232.00	287.68	287.68
6518	-	99	-	Alton	Alton	515.20	638.85	-
6519	-	135	-	Alton	Alton	360.00	446.40	-
6520	-	55	-	Alton	Alton	44.00	54.56	1139.81

1798 DIRECT TAX

Pg/No	Occupant Surname	Occupant First Name	Owner Surname	Owner First Name	Dwg #	Val $	Expt Acr
6521	Glidden	David	Glidden	David	-	-	-
6522	Glidden	John	Glidden	John	-	-	-
6523	-	-	Glidden	John	-	-	-
6524	Glidden	Phineas	Glidden	Phineas	-	-	-
6525	-	-	Hale	Samuel	-	-	-
6526	-	-	Haven	Samuel	-	-	-
6601	Hanson	Micaiah	Hanson	Micaiah	1	48	-
6602	-	-	Hanson	Micaiah	-	-	-
6603	Hayes	David	Hayes	David	1	16	-
6604	-	-	Hayes	Joseph	-	-	-
6605	Hill	Andrew W.	Hill	Jonathan	1	64	-
6606	Hayes	Paul	Hayes	Paul	-	-	-
6607	Hayes	Israel	Hayes	Paul	1	40	-
6608	Herds	Timothy	Herds	Timothy	1	64	-
6609	-	-	Herds	Timothy	-	-	-
6610	Horn	Paul	Horn	Paul	1	64	-
6611	-	-	Horn	Paul	-	-	-
6612	-	-	Jaffrey	George	-	-	-
6613	-	-	Jaffrey	George	-	-	-
6614	Wilkinson	James	Jewett	James	-	-	-
6615	Wooster	James	Jewett	James	-	-	-
6616	Hayes	Jonathan	Jewett	James	-	-	-
6617	-	-	Jewett	Thomas	-	-	-
6618	-	-	Joy	Samuel	-	-	-
6619	-	-	Jones	Joseph	-	-	-
6620	Jones	Isaac	Jones	Isaac	1	24	-
6621	-	-	Jones	Samuel	-	-	-
6622	Kimbal	Daniel	Kimbal	Daniel	1	48	-
6623	Knight	Joseph	Knight	Joseph	1	64	-
6624	-	-	Langdon	Woodbury	-	-	-
6625	-	-	Langdon	Woodbury	-	-	-
6626	-	-	Langdon	Woodbury	-	-	-
6701	Leighton	Jonathan	Leighton	Jonathan	1	64	-
6702	Leighton	Jonathan, Jr.	Leighton	Jonathan. Jr.	1	56	-
6703	Libbey	Abraham	Libbey	Abraham	1	24	-
6704	Lock	James	Lock	James	-	-	-
6705	McCluer	Samuel	McCluer	Samuel	-	-	-
6706	McDuffee	Daniel	McDuffee	Daniel	-	-	-
6707	-	-	McDuffee	Daniel	-	-	-
6708	-	-	McDuffee	Daniel	-	-	-
6709	Perkins	Ephraim	McDuffee	Daniel	1	-	-
6710	McDuffee	James	McDuffee	James	-	-	-
6711	-	-	McDuffee	James	-	-	-
6712	McDuffee	Jonathan	McDuffee	Jonathan	-	-	-
6713	-	-	McDuffee	Jonathan	-	-	-
6714	-	-	McDuffee	Jonathan	-	-	-
6715	-	-	McDuffee	Jonathan	-	-	-

NEW HAMPSHIRE DISTRICT 13

Pg/No	Ext Per	Acr	Per	Property Location	Residence of Owner	Value $	Eq. Val $	Total $
6521	-	99	-	Alton	Alton	475.20	589.25	589.25
6522	-	99	-	Alton	Alton	507.20	628.93	-
6523	-	84	-	Alton	Alton	67.20	83.32	712.25
6524	-	100	-	Alton	Alton	400.00	496.00	496.00
6525	-	300	-	Alton	Portsmouth	120.00	148.80	148.80
6526	-	200	-	Alton	Portsmouth	106.40	131.94	131.94
6601	-	99	-	Alton	Alton	480.00	595.20	-
6602	-	30	-	Alton	Alton	48.00	59.52	654.72
6603	-	150	-	Alton	Alton	648.00	803.52	803.52
6604	-	112	-	Alton	Barrington	569.60	706.30	706.30
6605	-	325	-	Alton	Gilmanton	624.00	773.76	773.76
6606	-	593	-	Alton	Alton	2033.60	2521.67	-
6607	-	200	-	Alton	Alton	872.00	1081.28	3602.95
6608	-	100	-	Alton	Alton	280.00	347.20	-
6609	-	50	-	Alton	Alton	80.00	99.20	446.40
6610	-	50	-	Alton	Alton	320.00	396.80	-
6611	-	50	-	Alton	Alton	40.00	49.60	446.40
6612	-	265	-	Alton	Portsmouth	212.00	262.88	-
6613	-	43	-	Alton	Portsmouth	23.20	28.77	291.65
6614	-	159	-	Alton	Dover	480.00	595.20	-
6615	-	199	-	Alton	Dover	1000.00	1240.00	-
6616	-	99	-	Alton	Dover	440.00	545.60	2380.80
6617	-	50	-	Alton	Alton	40.00	49.60	49.60
6618	-	200	-	Alton	Durham	106.40	131.94	131.94
6619	-	100	-	Alton	Rochester	280.00	347.20	347.20
6620	-	150	-	Alton	Alton	560.00	694.40	694.40
6621	-	100	-	Alton	Rochester	60.00	74.40	74.40
6622	-	100	-	Alton	Alton	304.00	376.96	376.96
6623	-	103	-	Alton	Alton	532.00	659.68	659.68
6624	-	1000	-	Alton	Portsmouth	400.00	496.00	-
6625	-	300	-	Alton	Portsmouth	240.00	297.60	-
6626	-	43	-	Alton	Portsmouth	23.20	28.76	822.36
6701	-	100	-	Alton	Alton	656.00	813.44	813.44
6702	-	35	-	Alton	Alton	140.00	173.60	173.60
6703	-	50	-	Alton	Alton	144.00	178.56	178.56
6704	-	90	-	Alton	Barnstead	288.00	357.12	357.12
6705	-	60	-	Alton	Alton	240.00	297.60	297.60
6706	-	99	80	Alton	Alton	264.00	327.36	-
6707	-	76	-	Alton	Alton	204.80	253.95	-
6708	-	150	-	Alton	Alton	60.00	74.40	655.71
6709	-	91	-	Alton	Rochester	448.00	555.52	555.52
6710	-	219	-	Alton	Alton	940.00	1165.60	-
6711	-	64	-	Alton	Alton	102.40	126.98	1292.58
6712	-	219	-	Alton	Alton	948.00	1175.52	-
6713	-	70	-	Alton	Alton	112.00	138.88	-
6714	-	250	-	Alton	Alton	200.00	248.00	-
6715	-	30	-	Alton	Alton	120.00	148.80	-

1798 DIRECT TAX

Pg/No	Occupant Surname	Occupant First Name	Owner Surname	Owner First Name	Dwg #	Val $	Expt Acr
6716	-	-	McDuffee	Jonathan	-	-	-
6717	McDuffee	William	McDuffee	William	1	32	-
6718	-	-	Martin	Thomas	-	-	-
6719	-	-	Martin	Thomas	-	-	-
6720	Meder	Moses	Meder	Moses	-	-	-
6721	-	-	Mellen	Henry	-	-	-
6722	Moores	Jonathan	Moores	Jonathan	-	-	-
6723	Morrison	David	Morrison	David	-	-	-
6724	-	-	Page	Benjamin	-	-	-
6725	Peavey	Oliver	Peavey	Oliver	-	-	-
6726	-	-	Peavey	Oliver	-	-	-
6801	-	-	Peirce	John	-	-	-
6802	-	-	Peirce	John	-	-	-
6803	Peirce	Joseph	Peirce	Joseph	-	-	-
6804	Pinkham	Clement	Peirce	Joseph	1	64	-
6805	Unimproved	-	Peirce	Joseph	-	-	-
6806	Unimproved	-	Peirce	Joseph	-	-	-
6807	Unimproved	-	Peirce	Joseph	-	-	-
6808	Unimproved	-	Peirce	Joseph	-	-	-
6809	Unimproved	-	Peirce	Joseph	-	-	-
6810	Unimproved	-	Peirce	Joseph	-	-	-
6811	Perkins	Thomas	Perkins	Thomas	-	-	-
6812	Place	Ebenezer	Place	Ebenezer	-	-	-
6813	-	-	Peirce	Peter	-	-	-
6814	-	-	Pinkham	Thomas	-	-	-
6815	-	-	Pinkham	Thomas	-	-	-
6816	-	-	Pinkham	Thomas	-	-	-
6817	Rawlings	John	Rawlings	John	1	48	-
6818	Rawlings	Ichabod	Rawlings	Ichabod	-	-	-
6819	Roberts	Joseph, Jr.	Roberts	Joseph, Jr.	-	-	-
6820	Roberts	Silas	Roberts	Silas	-	-	-
6821	-	-	Rogers	Charles	-	-	-
6822	McDuffee	Daniel	Rogers	Daniel	-	-	-
6823	Rogers	Samuel	Rogers	Samuel	1	40	-
6824	-	-	Runnals	Samuel	-	-	-
6825	Small	Joseph	Small	Joseph	-	-	-
6826	Smith	Josiah	Smith	Josiah	-	-	-
6901	Smith	Reuben	Smith	Reuben	-	-	-
6902	-	-	Sawyer	Enoch	-	-	-
6903	Stockbridge	David	Stockbridge	David	1	16	-
6904	Smith	Robinson	Smith	Robinson	-	-	-
6905	Stockbridge	Israel	Stockbridge	Israel	-	-	-
6906	Thurston	Josiah	Thurston	Josiah	-	-	-
6907	Unimproved	-	Unknown	-	-	-	-
6908	Unimproved	-	Unknown	-	-	-	-
6909	Unimproved	-	Unknown	-	-	-	-
6910	Unimproved	-	Unknown	-	-	-	-

NEW HAMPSHIRE DISTRICT 13

Pg/No	Ext Per	Acr	Per	Property Location	Residence of Owner	Value $	Eq. Val $	Total $
6716	-	64	-	Alton	Alton	102.40	126.97	1838.17
6717	-	92	-	Alton	Alton	497.60	617.02	617.02
6718	-	412	80	Alton	Portsmouth	164.80	204.35	-
6719	-	250	-	Alton	Portsmouth	200.00	248.00	452.35
6720	-	179	-	Alton	Alton	429.60	532.71	532.71
6721	-	130	-	Alton	Alton	208.00	257.92	257.92
6722	-	140	-	Alton	Alton	264.00	327.36	327.36
6723	-	180	-	Alton	Alton	464.00	575.36	575.36
6724	-	200	-	Alton	Gilmanton	400.00	496.00	496.00
6725	-	149	-	Alton	Alton	480.00	595.20	-
6726	-	50	-	Alton	Alton	40.00	49.60	644.80
6801	-	412	80	Alton	Portsmouth	164.80	204.35	-
6802	-	660	-	Alton	Portsmouth	352.00	436.48	640.83
6803	-	9	80	Alton	Alton	104.80	129.95	-
6804	-	100	-	Alton	Alton	576.00	714.24	-
6805	-	77	29	Alton	Alton	123.40	153.02	-
6806	-	750	-	Alton	Alton	600.00	744.00	-
6807	-	43	-	Alton	Alton	18.00	22.32	-
6808	-	43	-	Alton	Alton	18.00	22.32	-
6809	-	100	-	Alton	Alton	80.00	99.20	-
6810	-	100	-	Alton	Alton	32.00	39.68	1924.73
6811	-	100	-	Alton	Alton	80.00	99.20	99.20
6812	-	40	-	Alton	Alton	128.00	158.72	158.72
6813	-	200	-	Alton	Portsmouth	106.00	131.44	131.44
6814	-	100	-	Alton	Durham	80.00	99.20	-
6815	-	100	-	Alton	Durham	80.00	99.20	-
6816	-	100	-	Alton	Durham	80.00	99.20	297.60
6817	-	160	-	Alton	Alton	400.00	496.00	496.00
6818	-	58	-	Alton	Alton	128.80	159.71	159.71
6819	-	100	-	Alton	Alton	360.00	446.40	446.40
6820	-	29	-	Alton	Alton	180.80	224.19	224.19
6821	-	76	-	Alton	Alton	121.60	150.79	150.79
6822	-	99	80	Alton	Rochester	264.00	327.36	327.36
6823	-	144	-	Alton	Alton	640.00	793.60	793.60
6824	-	150	-	Alton	New Durham	60.00	74.40	74.40
6825	-	199	80	Alton	Alton	480.00	595.20	595.20
6826	-	60	-	Alton	Alton	240.00	297.60	297.60
6901	-	149	80	Alton	Alton	359.20	445.41	445.41
6902	-	1	-	Alton	Alton	40.00	49.60	49.60
6903	-	60	-	Alton	Alton	208.00	257.92	257.92
6904	-	100	-	Alton	Alton	320.00	396.80	396.80
6905	-	99	-	Alton	Alton	536.00	664.64	664.64
6906	-	100	-	Alton	Alton	320.00	396.80	396.80
6907	-	300	-	Alton	Alton	160.00	198.40	198.40
6908	-	43	-	Alton	Unknown	23.20	28.77	28.77
6909	-	776	-	Alton	Unknown	620.00	768.80	768.80
6910	-	300	-	Alton	Unknown	160.00	198.40	198.40

1798 DIRECT TAX

Pg/No	Occupant Surname	Occupant First Name	Owner Surname	Owner First Name	Dwg #	Val $	Expt Acr
6911	Unimproved	-	Unknown	-	-	-	-
6912	Unimproved	-	Unknown	-	-	-	-
6913	Unimproved	-	Unknown	-	-	-	-
6914	Unimproved	-	Unknown	-	-	-	-
6915	Unimproved	-	Unknown	-	-	-	-
6916	Unimproved	-	Unknown	-	-	-	-
6917	Unimproved	-	Unknown	-	-	-	-
6918	Unimproved	-	Unknown	-	-	-	-
6919	Unimproved	-	Unknown	-	-	-	-
6920	Unimproved	-	Unknown	-	-	-	-
6921	Unimproved	-	Unknown	-	-	-	-
6922	Unimproved	-	Unknown	-	-	-	-
6923	Unimproved	-	Unknown	-	-	-	-
6924	Unimproved	-	Unknown	-	-	-	-
6925	Unimproved	-	Unknown	-	-	-	-
6926	Unimproved	-	Unknown	-	-	-	-
7001	Unimproved	-	Unknown	-	-	-	-
7002	Unimproved	-	Unknown	-	-	-	-
7003	Unimproved	-	Unknown	-	-	-	-
7004	Unimproved	-	Unknown	-	-	-	-
7005	Unimproved	-	Unknown	-	-	-	-
7006	Unimproved	-	Unknown	-	-	-	-
7007	Unimproved	-	Unknown	-	-	-	-
7008	Unimproved	-	Unknown	-	-	-	-
7009	Unimproved	-	Unknown	-	-	-	-
7010	Unimproved	-	Unknown	-	-	-	-
7011	Unimproved	-	Unknown	-	-	-	-
7012	Unimproved	-	Unknown	-	-	-	-
7013	Unimproved	-	Unknown	-	-	-	-
7014	Unimproved	-	Unknown	-	-	-	-
7015	Unimproved	-	Unknown	-	-	-	-
7016	Unimproved	-	Unknown	-	-	-	-
7017	Unimproved	-	Unknown	-	-	-	-
7018	Unimproved	-	Unknown	-	-	-	-
7019	Unimproved	-	Waldron	John	-	-	-
7020	Unimproved	-	Waldron	John	-	-	-
7021	Unimproved	-	Waldron	John	-	-	-
7022	Walker	George	Walker	George	1	48	-
7023	Wentworth	Ebenezer	Wentworth	Ebenezer	1	24	-
7024	Woodman	Jeremiah	Woodman	Jeremiah	-	-	-
7025	-	-	Woodman	Jeremiah	-	-	-
7026	Weeks	Noah	Weeks	Noah	-	-	-

NEW HAMPSHIRE DISTRICT 13

Pg/No	Ext Per	Acr	Per	Property Location	Residence of Owner	Value $	Eq. Val $	Total $
6911	-	950	-	Alton	Unknown	760.00	942.40	942.40
6912	-	100	-	Alton	Unknown	53.60	66.46	66.46
6913	-	220	-	Alton	Unknown	117.60	145.82	145.82
6914	-	220	-	Alton	Unknown	117.60	145.82	145.82
6915	-	40	-	Alton	Unknown	32.00	39.68	39.68
6916	-	40	-	Alton	Unknown	32.00	39.68	39.68
6917	-	222	-	Alton	Unknown	166.60	206.69	206.69
6918	-	150	-	Alton	Unknown	120.00	148.80	148.80
6919	-	213	-	Alton	Unknown	170.40	211.30	211.30
6920	-	216	-	Alton	Unknown	172.80	214.27	214.27
6921	-	500	-	Alton	Unknown	266.40	330.33	330.33
6922	-	100	-	Alton	Unknown	53.60	66.46	66.46
6923	-	166	-	Alton	Unknown	88.80	110.12	110.12
6924	-	500	-	Alton	Unknown	266.40	330.33	330.33
6925	-	125	-	Alton	Unknown	50.00	62.00	62.00
6926	-	43	-	Alton	Unknown	23.20	28.77	28.77
7001	-	317	-	Alton	Unknown	253.60	314.46	314.46
7002	-	396	-	Alton	Unknown	211.20	261.89	261.89
7003	-	43	-	Alton	Unknown	23.20	28.77	28.77
7004	-	1000	-	Alton	Unknown	400.00	496.00	496.00
7005	-	100	-	Alton	Unknown	40.00	49.60	49.60
7006	-	365	-	Alton	Unknown	196.00	243.04	243.04
7007	-	350	-	Alton	Unknown	280.00	347.20	347.20
7008	-	125	-	Alton	Unknown	50.00	62.00	62.00
7009	-	43	-	Alton	Unknown	23.20	28.77	28.77
7010	-	288	-	Alton	Unknown	230.40	285.69	285.69
7011	-	43	-	Alton	Unknown	23.20	28.77	28.77
7012	-	1100	-	Alton	Unknown	587.20	728.13	728.13
7013	-	90	-	Alton	Unknown	48.00	59.52	59.52
7014	-	220	-	Alton	Unknown	117.60	145.82	145.82
7015	-	165	-	Alton	Unknown	88.00	109.12	109.12
7016	-	43	-	Alton	Unknown	23.20	28.77	28.77
7017	-	43	-	Alton	Unknown	23.20	28.77	28.77
7018	-	43	-	Alton	Unknown	23.20	28.77	28.77
7019	-	200	-	Alton	Dover	240.00	297.60	-
7020	-	100	-	Alton	Dover	120.00	148.80	-
7021	-	130	-	Alton	Dover	208.00	257.92	704.32
7022	-	150	-	Alton	Alton	608.00	753.92	753.92
7023	-	100	-	Alton	Alton	440.00	545.60	545.60
7024	-	99	80	Alton	Alton	350.40	434.50	-
7025	-	20	-	Alton	Alton	32.00	39.68	474.18
7026	-	40	-	Alton	Alton	128.00	158.72	158.72

SURNAME INDEX

Abbot..32,80
Adams..10,24,80
Allard..10,24,32,54,70
Allen..10,12,24,40
Ambrose..82
Ames..82
Babb..40
Baker..14,54,60
Ballard.12,40
Banfield..60
Barker..70
Bassett..10,24
Beacham..82
Bean..18,92,94
Beck..76
Been..32
Bennett..16,18,54,60,70,92
Berry..16,70
Bickford..10,16,24,32,70,72,82
Blake..10,24,82
Blasdel..12,40
Blazo..60
Blydenburgh..70
Boardman..40
Boody..16,54,72
Bowles..72
Brackett..24,82
Bradbury..60
Brewster..10,24
Brown..10,14,18,24,28,32,38,
       40,54,60,82,92
Bryant..40,60
Bunker..72
Burbank..32
Burk..54
Burleigh..12,40,82
Burnham..72
Buzzell..18,50,60,82,92
Calder..12,14,54
Calley..60
Camey..82
Canney..16,32,72
Carr..92
Carter..82
Cate..24,54
Caverly..72
Chamberlain..14,16,18,24,42,54
            72,92
Chapman..12,40

Chappotin..14,54
Chase..10,24
Chesley..50,72
Chick..82
Clark..12,40,42,50,72
Clay..14,54
Clements..92
Clemmont..24
Clifford..24
Clough..18,92,94
Cloutman..12,42
Coffin..18,94
Cogswell..16,42,76,94
Colbath..50
Colby..42
Coleman..14,24,56
Colomy..16,50,72
Connor..10,24
Cook..12,14,42,50
Cooley..82
Cooper..60
Copp..10,12,24.32,34,42,56 82
Costellow..60
Cotton..10,24,60
Cram..60
Cross..60
Cutter..24
Cutts..42
Dame, Jr...34
Daniels..56
Davis..14,16,18,50,72,74,94
Dearborn..12,14,34,42,60,62,82
Deeling..56
Deering..74
Demeritt..82
Dodge..18,82
Doe..60,74
Dore..82
Dow..12,42,82
Drake..16,62
Drew..14,16,24,50,56,74,76
Drown..74
Ducoin..74
Dudley..18,94
Durgan..16,50,56,74,76
Dutton..94
Eaton..94
Edgerly..16,42,56,74.76,94
Edmonds..24,26

-103-

SURNAME INDEX

Eldridge..82
Elkins..16,74,94
Ellis..50,74,82
Emerson..62,82
Emery..34
Estes..10,24
Evans..24,34,74,94
Fall..94
Fellows..42
Fernald..10,14,26,56
Fisher..18,62,94
Flanders..18,94
Fogg..18,82
Folsom..16,18,26,42,76,82,94
Footman..50
Foss..34
Fox..26
French..16,34,76,94
Frost..10,14,26,50
Fullerton..10,26
Furber..10,26
Gage..42,50,56
Garland..12,42,82
Garlin..50
Garvin..42
Gerrish..50
Giles..56
Gilman..12,18,42,56,76,82,84,94
Glidden..18,62,84,96
Glover..26
Glyn..26
Goddard..34
Goldsmith..26,84
Goldthwait..34
Goodal..76
Gore..26
Goudy..84
Gould..28
Grant..84
Graves..12,34,84
Grover..26
Guppy..14,26,56
Hacket..14,56
Haines..10,12,26,44
Hale..96
Haley..34,84
Hall..12,34,42,44,56,62
Hamons..76

Hanson..12,14,18,34,44,50,56,76,84,96
Hardy..10,12,26,44,50
Harmons..76
Haven..34,36,96
Hawkins..44
Hayes..18,76,84,96
Heirn..62
Heix..50
Herds..96
Hersey..10,26
Hide..10,26,84
Hill..44,96
Hiner..14,50,76
Hobbs..16,62
Hodgdon..26,34,44,50,84
Hodge..14,56
Holmes..34
Horn..10,12,26,34,44,50,56,96
Horsam..84
Huggin..44
Hurd..44
Hutchens..12,44
Jackson..16,76
Jaffrey..16,26,50,56,62,76,96
Jenkins..76
Jenness..26
Jennings..16,76
Jewett..10,18,26,76,96
Johnson..14,28,44,50,52,56,76
Jones..28,84,96
Joy..16,76,96
Judkins..26
Kelly..76
Kennison..14,28,36,44,52,56,76,84,88
Kenny..76
Kent..56,76
Key..28
Keys..84
Kimball..12,44,52,96
Kineson..16
Knight..18,76,84,96
Lamper..62,64
Lane..10,28
Lang..12,44
Langdon..36,38,96
Lary..28
Lear..28,84

SURNAME INDEX

Leavitt..12,16,28,36,44,62,64,84
Lee..36
Leighton..16,52,76,84,96
Libbey..10,28,36,56,76,96
Lindsey..12,44
Littlefield..64
Lock..44,96
Lord..16,64,76,84
Lucas..28
Lyford..14,56
Mailham..12,44
Mallard..38
Maloon..64
Manning..12,44
Marden..26,28,38
Marsh..44
Marston..16,64
Martin..14,28,56,98
Mason..76,84
Mathes..76
McCluer..96
McDuffee..18,20,96,98
McIntire..38
Meader..38
Meder..10,28,98
Mellen..98
Meloon..38
Merrow..44
Meserve..76
Mitchel..76
Moffatt..38
Moody..28,38,84
Mooney..16,76
Moores..98
Mordough..12,46
Morgan..64
Morrison..18,98
Moulton..16,46,52,64
Murray..76
Nay..18,84
Neal..12,28,46
Nickerson..84
Nock..84
Norris..28
Norton..76
Nowell..28
Noys..64
Nudd..12,28,46

Nute..28,38
Nutt..28
Nutter..38,80,84
Page..40,46,66,94,98
Palmer..12,28,46,52,56,64,76
Paul..46
Pearl..76
Pearson..66
Peavey..20,38,78,98
Peirce..20,28,38,40,84,98
Penhallow..28,52
Perkins..12,28,38,46,52,56,76,84,96,98
Philbrick..12,16,46,64,66
Pike..14,46,52,56
Pinkham..18,40,66,94,98
Piper..12,28,38,40,46,52
Pitman..66,86
Place..50,98
Poland..18,86
Pottle..52
Prebble..86
Quarles..86
Quimby..46
Rawlings..98
Reed..28
Rendall..40
Richards..52,56
Richardson..46
Ricker..56
Rindge..30
Roberts..16,46,52,78,86,98
Robinson..14,40,56
Rogers..10,20,28,30,86,98
Roles..86
Rundlet..46
Runnals..16,52,78,98
Rust..10,30
Safford..46
Sanborn..14,46,56
Sanderson..86
Savage..80
Sawyer..14,98
Sayer..14,58
Scates..46
Seammon..14,46
Seavey..30
Serjeant..30
Shannon..46

SURNAME INDEX

Shaw..78
Sheafe..30,40
Sherborne..46,58
Shorey..30
Shortridge..30
Sias..18,86
Siedgal..86
Skinner..14,46
Small..20,98
Smart..86
Smith..10,18,20,30,32,52,78,
  84,86,98
Snell..30
Stanton..14,52,58
Staple..86
Steel..66
Stevens..16,40,52,78
Stewart..78
Stockbridge..20,98
Stodard..14,58
Suthern..30
Swain..78
Swasey..30,66
Sweat..40
Tash..16,52,58,78
Tasker..14,60,86
Taylor..16,40,66,78,86
Thing..40,86
Thomas..40,52,78
Thompson..58
Thurston..10,30,46,98
Tibbets..10,14,30,58,66,78
Titcomb..16,66
Towle..66,86
Townsend..10,30
Trask..10,30
Treadwell..30

Trickey..52,58
Triggs..10,30
Tucker..30,86
Tuttle..58
Twambly..54
Twombly..54
Varney..30,32,66,78
Verney..10
Waldron..100
Walker..100
Ward..66
Warren..10,32,40
Watson..14,46,48,58,78
Wedgwood..66
Weeks..14,48,100
Welch..14,48,66,86
Wentworth..32,48,58,76,86,100
Whipple..40
White..86
Whitehouse..14,40,54,58
Whitten..32
Whittle..10,32
Wiggin..12,14,32,40,48,58
Wilkinson..18,96
Willard..58
Wille..16,18,28,32,34,40,58,
  78,80
Wingate..14,48,54
Witham..48
Woodman..20,52,100
Wooster..18,96
Wormwood..32
Yeaton..32
York..54
Young..12,14,18,32,40,48,66,
  78,80,86,94

www.ingramcontent.com/pod-product-compliance
Lightning Source LLC
Chambersburg PA
CBHW080406170426
43193CB00016B/2829